DEVOTIONAL COMMENTARY

THE
Joshua
Generation

*a 40-day journey into
your promised land*

Brian & Candice Simmons

BroadStreet
PUBLISHING

BroadStreet Publishing® Group, LLC
Savage, Minnesota, USA
BroadStreetPublishing.com

The Joshua Generation: A 40-Day Journey into Your Promised Land
Copyright © 2023 Brian Simmons

9781424565283 (softcover)
9781424565290 (ebook)

Stock or custom editions of BroadStreet Publishing titles may be purchased in bulk for educational, business, ministry, fundraising, or sales promotional use. For information, please email orders@broadstreetpublishing.com.

Cover and interior by Garborg Design Works | garborgdesign.com

Printed in China

23 24 25 26 27 5 4 3 2 1

DEDICATION

To the new breed of courageous women and men,
a generation whose eyes are fixed on Jesus,
this book is affectionate dedicated.

Contents

INTRODUCTION

The season of God's mighty power has arrived! A new day has dawned, and with it comes the rising of a new breed of believers. This generation will carry the torch of truth in its hands. Mighty ones who will do his bidding are rising with grace in their hearts, humility in their lifestyles, and truth burning in their bones. This is the Joshua generation!

In this book, we'll dive heart deep into the study of one of the most amazing generations known in human history. And from this brave band of overcomers, you'll learn principles and truths that will help you now, in this generation, to fulfill your heavenly mandate and to possess your promised land. Joshua and Caleb were two faithful witnesses who refused to join in with others who gave a bad report after scouting out the land of Canaan. Instead, they believed the report of the Lord and defeated the enemy when others said that it couldn't be done. The other spies confessed that the giants of the land were too big and the enemy too strong. But Joshua and Caleb brought back a different report, God's report.

This is where breakthrough starts. It starts with God and his report. We must trust what he has said and move out in faith. And it must be a faith that refuses to back down and fit in with the nay-saying crowd. Breakthrough comes when we believe the report of the Lord.

You have that same Spirit in you. The Holy Spirit inside of you is saying, *If God says I can have it, then I'll have it. In fact, I must have it! There may be giants in my path, but they're no match for the overcomer inside of me. God is living within me, and he is my Breakthrough. Every promise in the book is mine, and I will not be denied, for I believe them and him.*

Sadly enough, even in the church, there are those who confess belief but speak a faithless, bad report. No matter what evil we see or what difficulties may come, God is going to bring revival. He has a plan, and it's to turn our nation back to God. Too many of us wimp out, give up, and take the low road of agreement with hell while heaven is calling us to a higher perspective. Jesus is at our side, and the cloud of witnesses is cheering us on. We're surrounded and supported by greatness.

I'm afraid most of us live on a mere fraction of God's blessing, but there is a spiritual bank account that is available for the people of God. Sadly, we're living under the spiritual poverty line most of the time. We often live in the realm of "not enough." Do you ever catch yourself saying, *I hope I make it; I hope I can get through this struggle; I hope I can walk through this issue*? This is the reverse of what God has destined for this glorious generation.

I prophesy to you: there is a generation rising on the earth today that will not sit in Laodicea any longer. They will not rest in a passive, lukewarm spirit. They will march out. They will cross the river Jordan, even at flood stage. They will carry the ark of God's glory. They will walk under the authority of heaven, and they will conquer every walled city and every foe that stands in their way. As God put it—let me quote the words of God himself—"Every part of the land where you march I will give you," says the Lord (Joshua 1:3). I believe you are reading this book right now so that you will be inspired to become *spiritually aggressive* in the things of God. His strength in us is restored, renewed, and released as we wait on him, believe his word, and trust everything that he's written for us. This is the faith journey you were created for. All the blessings of Abraham are yours, and every promise is yours.

It's time for you to enter into and possess all that God has given you in Christ. This forty-day journey through the story of the Joshua generation will take you from being a wanderer to becoming a warrior. So, let's begin this wonderful study of the Joshua generation, a company of overcomers, and let's be mantled with the understanding that God is with us. And he will equip us to do all that he's called us to do. Like Joshua's army, we cannot fail with God on our side.

LET'S PRAY

Father, ignite a greater faith in me for miracles and breakthroughs. Remove my unbelief and fill me with the holy confidence that you are all I need. God, I come running to you for strength, wisdom, and perseverance for the days to come. I want to be a part of the new breed that you are raising up on the earth today. I offer myself to you. Give me the courage of Joshua as I set my heart before you. Amen.

I

THE BOOK OF JOSHUA: OUR ROAD MAP

Joshua is the sixth book of the Bible. It begins the section of history in the Word of God known as the "Former Prophets." Bundled together, Joshua through Esther give us a road map. Joshua teaches us how to move forward with courage to conquer our giants of unbelief and shows us the secrets of possessing our land, our promised inheritance, and our destiny. It's our road map to victory.

The author of Joshua, of course, is Joshua. His name can mean "YAHWEH is Savior" or "the salvation of YAHWEH." In fact, the name Joshua is the virtual Hebrew equivalent of the word Jesus. So, this book could be called the book of Jesus—Yeshua!

Moses could not take the people into the promised land, but Jesus can. Moses represents the law, and the law is powerless to deliver the heart of man (see Romans 8:3). With the law, we get stuck in our wilderness, but Jesus (Joshua) is the overcomer. He's the one who can break us free from the wildernesses of our lives. He can break through every stronghold and every barrier. And Jesus will be the one to bring us in.

Joshua contains the story of how God brought the people of Israel out of their wilderness wanderings. It reveals how YAHWEH watched over his people as they faced warfare all around them. It, therefore, becomes a manual for spiritual warfare for all those who desire to possess their destiny.

With a new day there are always new strategies. One generation passes, and another one arises. And a new generation signals a new beginning. Some of us have been wandering around so long that our sandals and sneakers are worn out. We're busting our shoestrings, breaking our heels, and wearing holes in our soles. We've got to get out of the place of wandering and come into the place of glory where the power of God flows.

HEAVEN ON EARTH

Moses was gone, and Joshua was left with the task of leading the people into a new beginning. It was time, a God setup. God had a new and different plan for Joshua. And his plan was to bring the people to a place that God called heaven on earth.

> Therefore shall ye lay up these my words in your heart and in your soul…That your days may be multiplied, and the days of your children, in the land which the LORD sware unto your fathers to give them, as the days of heaven upon the earth. (Deuteronomy 11:18, 21 KJV)

God's intention for Israel in the promised land was to give them a foretaste of heaven. And this heaven was more than a place in the sweet by and by. It was the realm of God where we walked in victory and supernatural power. The promised land was literally heaven on earth.

How would you like to go there? How would you like to go into a new season in your life where depression is gone and relationship tensions are over? Suddenly there's grace on you, and you can walk in buoyancy and freedom you've not known before, a glorious realm of heaven touching the earth. Would you like that? The church needs the message of the book of Joshua more than ever before. We're living in a day when many of God's people are walking in defeat and discouragement. But God's destiny for every one of us is that we shine "fair as the shining moon, bright and brilliant as the sun in all its strength—astonishing to behold as a majestic army waving banners of victory" (Song of Songs 6:10). Today is the time to come out of hiding. We'll no longer live like prisoners of war, for we were never made to hide as captives. But we are meant to rise up as a Joshua Company.

MENTORED BY MOSES

Joshua was mentored and raised up by Moses. Like Joshua, we, too, must recognize the benefits of drawing from the wisdom of the preceding generation. They have so much that they can teach us. Sometimes it takes a humbling of our heart to realize it, but it's worth it. A know-it-all spirit will take us nowhere fast. Our fathers have gone before us and plowed the way, and one day we'll look back and realize that we owe much of our success to them. To make the greatest impact on the world, we can't afford to ignore what has already been built. And the sooner we build on the foundation of those who have gone before, the sooner we'll have success. It will be to our detriment if we don't. We need to respect those who have gone before and add to what they have built.

Joshua, Moses' assistant (see Joshua 1:1), learned the things of God as he walked with Moses. Elisha walked with Elijah, and the disciples walked with Jesus. And so, in the local church, God sets elders in place. He puts them in places of leadership so that they become holy mentors of others. We can learn from the rich treasures that have gone before us and take the wisdom of the fathers and mothers even further on. And by our example, we can teach a whole new generation about honoring, humbling our hearts, and being mentored. Are you willing to learn and to honor those over you? Or are you convinced that the older generation doesn't have anything to give? If you believe the latter, you're missing out.

Let's Pray

Almighty God, Lord Eternal, lead me forward. I don't want to remain locked into my past or frozen with fear over what may come. Feed me the bread of champions. Give me eyes that see how great and powerful you are. Conquer every fear that hides in my heart. I know I can never arise and succeed without you, so give me your might and strength today. Amen.

2

DESTINY MARCHES ON

Leaders come and go, but the purpose, calling, and destiny of the church marches on. There's a purpose that is bigger and greater than any leader or group of leaders. Yes, we need leaders. We need authentic, apostolic men and women who are fathers and mothers that lead us by example. We always need them. We need the Billy Grahams, the Jonathan Edwardses, the Kathryn Kuhlmans, the Charles Finneys, the William Seymours, the Dwight Moodys, the Maria Woodworth-Etters, the Evan Robertses. But leaders pass away, and we don't have them forever. And new generations must take their place.

In the beginning of the book of Joshua, Moses, the hero and great leader, had died, and now the biggest challenge for Joshua had come. It was time for *him* to arise and take Moses' place. Joshua couldn't move out on Moses' revelation. Moses' revelation was yesterday's revelation. Joshua had to have a new and fresh revelation that the Father had for him to move into.

The book of Joshua is a picture of the rising of a modern-day company of men and women who will be carrying the cross and resurrection power of Christ. Their goal will be to take possession of age-old foundations while conquering the strongholds of darkness. They will take back the things that have been stolen from us, like our true identity in Christ and our true destiny in his glory. It's time for us to possess the healing gifts of God, the power gifts that release signs and wonders. Just like it was in the book of Acts, we need to see God's power multiplied on earth again. For God's people are arising, and we will demonstrate the glory of God and his power as we speak in his name.

NEW LEADERSHIP

The book of Joshua begins with God's divine commissioning of Joshua into leadership. For whenever God brings a new beginning, he raises up new leadership to initiate it. When we want to accomplish something, we begin by making our plans and strategies. We often look for a new method, a new, novel, clever way of doing it. But when God has something new and powerful that he wants to accomplish, he always raises up people—a new breed of people. God's people are God's methods. The way God moves on earth is through us. And as we mature and arise as a generation that seeks his face, we'll emerge in a victory that takes all that's waiting for us. As we believe his Word, his works will begin to flow through us, releasing the victory of Christ over the enemy and his plans for the earth.

Joshua 1:1–3 is the best example of a good generational transfer of leadership. Joshua had been mentored, submitted, and faithful to God and Moses. He had accompanied Moses and had won some battles, and in time, God promoted him and raised him up. And this is still the method that God uses to raise up leaders today.

Moses was one of the best leaders anyone could ever hope to be mentored by. What an honor that would've been! Joshua had been Moses' personal assistant. What an opportunity! Day in and day out, Joshua walked alongside a leader and leaders who heard from God and had devoted their lives to Yeshua. And as Joshua remained faithful to Moses and God, he was promoted and made ready for the transfer of leadership.

> After Moses, YAHWEH's servant, died, YAHWEH spoke to Joshua son of Nun, Moses' faithful assistant, and said, "My servant Moses is dead. Now get up! Prepare to cross the Jordan River, you and all the people. Lead them into the land that I am giving to the Israelites." (Joshua 1:1–2)

God chose Joshua—not Moses—to bring the Israelites into the promised land. And as it was with Joshua, God has a special calling for each and every man and every woman whom he loves. You, too, can bring glory to God as you fulfill God's purpose during your days here on earth. No two people have the same calling, so it's imperative that you hear God's plan for you personally and then commit to doing it faithfully.

Joshua started out as a slave in Egypt with all the "baggage" that comes with slavery. And like all the Israelites, he was delivered, but the sting and oppression of slavery lingered in his soul. He knew what it meant to be rejected and to feel inferior in culture and society. He had been marred and hurt by his experience, but God used it all to transform a slave into a champion.

You can imagine that Joshua may have been beaten. And no doubt he had worked in the hot sun and toiled for Pharaoh's kingdom. He was still a young man when he came out of Egypt, but his training for leadership began while working as a slave. God never wastes any part of our lives. Even the most tragic circumstances we walk through God will use for good (see Romans 8:28). The enemy may have meant it for evil, but the Father used it in Joshua to bring him into his promised inheritance and to bring glory and honor to God.

Joshua understood hardship. All he had gone through was preparation for becoming a courageous soldier. As the people of God began their journey through the wilderness, they had their first encounter with the people who were called the Amalekites.

> The Amalekites came and attacked the Israelites at Rephidim. Moses said to Joshua, "Choose some of our men and go out to fight the Amalekites. Tomorrow I will stand on top of the hill with the staff of God in my hands." (Exodus 17:8–9 NIV)

Real leaders are those who don't allow an attack to stop them. Moses put Joshua in charge, for he knew that Joshua wasn't one who would back down. No longer a slave, it was Joshua's day to arise. His struggle with the past was over, and he would no longer be oppressed. He was no longer a victim, and a revolutionary spirit was rising up within him. Great men and women of God are never quitters! They don't turn back. They'll stand up and say, "Even if everyone else quits, I'll press on. I refuse to give up and let the enemy take over!" And so, it's time for you to arise too. The words God spoke to Joshua, he is now speaking to you.

"I repeat, be strong and brave! Do not yield to fear nor be discouraged, for I am Yahweh your God, and I will be with you wherever you go!"[1]

Joshua ordered the leaders of the people: "Go through the camp and instruct the people, 'Pack your bags; for within three days you will cross the Jordan to conquer and occupy the land that Yahweh your God is giving you to possess!'" (Joshua 1:9–11)

Let's Pray

Father of Glory, I ask you to open the heavens over my heart and my home. I want to be filled with your divine purpose every moment of this day. I long to be close to you. As I draw near to you, draw near to me. I want to borrow your life, your strength, and your wisdom for the challenges I face. Mighty Warrior, I surrender to you. Amen.

3

Joshua the Servant

So far, we've seen Joshua as the slave and the soldier, but he was also a submitted servant. He gave his life and his future destiny into the hands of a leader—Moses. That can be a hard test for many. The woundedness of our life, the lack of fathering, and the lack of good role models in the church can become comfortable, convenient excuses to keep us from submitting our lives to others and from living a submitted lifestyle of loyalty, purity, and holiness. But until we can learn to submit to another person and his or her vision, it will be hard for God to bless us. For no matter who's over us, God is the ultimate authority, and he's the one who places men and women in positions of authority over us.

Joshua the Seeker

Joshua saw all this and learned from what he saw in Moses. While everybody else was doing their own thing, Joshua was watching Moses and the way he dealt with people, how he spoke in secret, in private, and in public. He watched as Moses prayed and God listened to his prayers, and before long, he began to absorb them. Joshua absorbed the same anointing as Moses. And he loved being in the glory just as Moses had. A Joshua generation will be the same way. They will break free of their slavery and become warriors for the kingdom. They will be holy, submitted servants who will do their best to obey even when they have restricting structures—such as their jobs or the pressures of the culture—over them, for in their heart of hearts, they will be seekers of God's glory.

> Now Moses used to take a tent and pitch it outside the camp some distance away, calling it the "tent of meeting." Anyone inquiring of the LORD would go to the tent of meeting outside the camp. And whenever Moses went out to the tent, all the people rose and stood at the entrances to their tents, watching Moses until he entered the tent. As Moses went into the tent, the pillar of cloud would come down and stay at the entrance, while the LORD spoke with Moses. Whenever the people saw the pillar of cloud standing at the entrance to the tent, they all stood and worshiped, each at the entrance to their tent. The LORD would speak to Moses face to face, as one speaks to a friend. Then Moses would return to the camp, but his young aide Joshua son of Nun did not leave the tent. (Exodus 33:7–11 NIV)

How close do you want to be with God? Both Moses and Joshua had no trouble with God the Father being close and in their faces. Moses was God's instrument. So, whenever Moses would return to the camp, he'd go right into the tent of meeting and spend time with the Father. Joshua also loved the presence of the Lord like Moses. When he went into the tent, he didn't want to leave. When Moses came out, Joshua remained.

There's something extra special about the Joshua generation. They go into the presence of the Lord, but they don't want to come out. They just stay right there. Others will say, "Oh well, it's time to go."

But the Joshua generation is full of passionate ones who will not be denied. They will live in his presence, and when they do go out, they will touch the masses with his glory, for they will carry it to the ends of the earth. Their hearts say, *I just want to worship. I just want to be in the place of his glowing, glistening, and burning presence. I want to radiate with his glory. I know God is here.*

JOSHUA THE SPY

Not only was Joshua a slave, a soldier, a servant, and a seeker, but he also was a spy. Another term for this would be *forerunner.* He went ahead to discover what God was doing. He was prophetic: a leader and a prophet. He had to see what was out there. I think he got this from Moses because Moses had to see what was out in the backside of the desert. And it was that encounter of hearing God speak out of the bush that really launched Moses' ministry.

Every leader is an explorer at heart because leaders always go beyond what they already know. They aren't just maintainers. They've got to move forward and go beyond. Maintainers will never reach the world. But the world will be reached by those with a mission burning in their hearts. They have a passion for seeing, going, and leading others into the unknown. There have to be adventurous ones, those who are like Joshua and go out as forerunners.

Joshua was a spy who developed strategies for the future. Militarily, he was an awesome general. He knew how to plot out the land of Canaan where the Philistines lived. First, he divided the land of the enemy in half. He used wise strategy over and over until he took nearly the entire land. But he failed to finish the job. So, he had to raise up judges (deliverers) to preside over the people who remained. Joshua was a city-reacher. To this day his military techniques are discussed in the halls of higher learning by the military strategists.

JOSHUA THE SUCCESSOR

Joshua was Moses' successor. Can you imagine being chosen to succeed Moses? He had some big shoes to fill. But he was ready, for he had received the anointing and the mantle as a result of his time before Jehovah God.

> The LORD said to Moses, "Take Joshua, son of Nun, a man in whom is the spirit of leadership, and lay your hand on him. Have him stand before Eleazar the priest and the entire assembly and commission him in their presence. Give him some of your authority so the whole Israelite community will obey him." (Numbers 27:18–20 NIV)

How awesome is this? The spirit of God was in Joshua to lead. "So now lay your hand on him, Moses. Give him some of your authority." In Joshua 1, God verbally commissioned Joshua to take Moses' place. And Joshua, Moses' successor, received the mantle of leadership through the laying on of hands. We, too, have been anointed to burst through barriers and soar into the adventurous, courageous life of faith.

LET'S PRAY

Father God, I need the courage that you can give me. I face difficulties, and sometimes they overwhelm me. Give me the grace and the courage to break through the barriers and limitations that surround me. I thank you today that my strength is renewed when I come into your presence. I take you with me, my God and my strength. I can do all things through the strength that you pour into my life today. Amen.

4

KEY STRATEGIES FOR
A NEW BREED

We can cross over the threshold to becoming an amazing generation of men and women, the Joshua generation! This brave band of overcomers will fulfill their heavenly mandate. A band of believers who believe the report of the Lord and will pursue it when all others turn and run.

Joshua and Caleb were the two faithful witnesses who would not be denied the land God had promised they would conquer. Everybody else said it couldn't be done. They all said that the giants were too big. The oppressive works of the enemy were too strong for the children of Israel. They were convinced that they would be defeated and that they couldn't break through. But Joshua and Caleb came back with a different report, a good report. For they were full of faith. And we can be full of faith too. We can be among those who will not be denied, those who press through until we find the breakthrough.

You have the Holy Spirit on the inside of you, saying to you right now, *If God says you can have it, then you can! There may be giants in your path, but they're no match for the overcomer on the inside of you. Every promise in the book is yours, and you will not be denied.*

In the church, there are those who believe yet speak a faithless and bad report. Don't listen to them. No matter what evil we see or what difficulties may come, God is going to bring revival. He's going to turn this nation back to God. Too many of us wimp out and take the low road of agreement with hell when heaven is calling us to a higher perspective. Jesus is at our side, and the great cloud of witnesses is cheering us on. We're surrounded and supported by greatness. We cannot fail, and we will not fail with God on our side.

KEY #1: REALIZE THE IMPORTANCE OF TRANSITION

You and I need a fresh beginning, so bury the past and seize the new. *Carpe diem!* Get free from the law with all of its law-keeping, guilt-driven theology, along with its shame, rejection, and inferiority. Moses died (Moses is a picture of the law), and only Joshua (Joshua is a picture of Jesus) can take us in. We need new leadership for our new day of victory. The Joshua type of leadership is more than any human being, religious structure, or new wineskin; it's Jesus. The law can never deliver the heart of man. You'll only get stuck in a wilderness, but Jesus is the overcomer. He's the one who breaks through every stronghold and every barrier. Jesus will bring us into our inheritance.

The first miracle of Moses was to turn the water of the Nile into blood. But the first miracle of Jesus (our heavenly Joshua) was to turn the water of Cana into *wine*. Now he wants to turn your water into wine.

One generation passes, and another generation rises. It's always that way. You've got to get out of that wandering place and come into the place of God's glory where the power of God flows. It's now your turn to arise and to go right on in. Leaders, even great leaders, come and go. We see a waterfall of great leaders cascading through church history. One man, one woman, one leader after another, they come and bless the church, but they pass on. God wasn't dead; only Moses was dead! But he raised up a Joshua underneath him to carry on. And so, the continual progression of God's purposes goes on, and wise is the man or woman who understands his or her place in this brief, momentary, fleeting life. We are but a vapor. And we all are like grass that grows for a brief season, and one day we all pass. But God's ways will remain eternally.

Key #2: Go for Your Promise of a Full Inheritance

> From the overflow of his fullness
> we received grace heaped upon more grace!
> Moses gave us the Law, but Jesus, the Anointed
> One, unveils truth wrapped in tender mercy.
> (John 1:16–17)

Joshua saw the need for a new beginning for his generation. For God wanted to bring the people into a place that he called heaven on earth. God doesn't want you to settle for a fraction when he is offering you fullness. God's intention for Israel in the promised land was to give them a foretaste of heaven. The promised land represents heaven on earth. It's the realm in God where we walk in his fullness, victory, and supernatural power. It's the realm where we claim every promise, step out in faith, and know that we can defeat the enemy. How would you like to step into that season right now? A season where suddenly there's a grace on your life to walk in buoyancy and freedom you've not previously known? It's the place where the glorious realm of heaven touches earth.

We're no longer prisoners of war, and we need to stop living that way. Joshua was a former slave, but he had to get rid of that slave mentality, and he became a soldier and a warrior. Like Joshua, you, too, were created to be a territory taker and a promise claimer. You've been created to walk in Christ's fullness and not in a partial victory. He's calling you to arise and take up his anointing. He's going to crown you with glory on your head instead of ashes. And he's going to crown you with rejoicing. The sadness of this generation is going to be broken by the jubilee of victory, the jubilee that comes with breaking through. Yes, Lord! We say yes!

LET'S PRAY

Father God, Mighty Warrior, and King of all the earth, I come and ask that you strengthen me with might in my inner being. Give me the warrior's wardrobe. Help me raise my shield of faith today and help me lay aside anything that would get in the way of my first love and devotion to you. I give you my heart, Lord God. Amen.

5

A New Day

It was said that David fulfilled the purpose of God in his generation (see Acts 13:36).[2] Don't you want it said of you that you are serving God's plan and not your own? God has a specific purpose for you too. Like David, you have certain tasks and responsibilities that God has chosen for you to fulfill. It is so important that each of us learns to hear God and seek to fulfill that purpose. Each of us should desire to finish our lives as faithful men and women of the gospel.

True visionaries will always look beyond a week, a month, a year. They investigate another realm. They go into the "decade mentality" of what they're going to do in the next ten years of their lives. Where do you want to be ten years from now? What do you want to see God accomplish on earth ten years from now? We've got to pull in through prayer and take the necessary steps to see it happen. Now, let's discover the third key strategy for the Joshua generation.

Key #3: Prepare to Lead People Forward

> Now get up! Prepare to cross the Jordan River, you
> and all the people. Lead them into the land that I
> am giving to the Israelites. (Joshua 1:2)

Get up! Prepare for a challenge. Lead the people into their inheritance. This was the exhortation God gave to Joshua. Did you see that God spoke to him? Every leader must hear God speak his plan for their lives, their families, and their ministries. Joshua got up and obeyed the voice of YAHWEH. Leaders will obey God.

So how did Joshua prepare himself for the challenge of crossing a flooding river? Although the Bible gives us few specifics, I am sure that Joshua humbled his heart before God and prayed for strength and courage to face the impossibility that was in front of him. And, I believe Joshua rested his heart in the promise of God, for God will never send you to do a task for him and let you fail. We only fail when we set out in our own strength to fulfill our own plans.

Indeed, Joshua knew deep in his soul that somehow, some-way, the river Jordan would have to move aside for God's people to pass. The Red Sea miracle was only forty years in their past. Joshua stood there and saw it with his own eyes. The waters split by the power of God, and the people crossed over on dry ground. Joshua remembered.

So how does a leader prepare for a challenge:

- Humble your heart before God.

- Acknowledge that only God can make a miracle happen.

- Rest your soul in the faith that moves mountains.

- Remember the miracles of your past. God will not let you down.

KEY #4: DON'T STOP TAKING NEW TERRITORY

Don't stop pressing forward. Ignore the words of others who tell you to give up and give in. Leaders may try to keep you locked into a limited vision. Good as they may be, and though their intentions may be pure in heart, you're the one who must ultimately answer to God. When the Lord speaks, we must follow.

If we're going to be a Joshua generation, we've got to take the land. We're not going to take the new territory with a limited vision. There's always more. God always has progressive revelation for us to press into. He goes from glory to glory. There are always bold new discoveries to be made. There's a realm out there that's a lot bigger than the greatest theological interpretation and list of doctrines that we can compile with our western mindset. My linear, western way of thinking isn't always going to take me to God. There's a bigger realm than the intellect. For the Bible says that the foolishness of God is "wiser than human wisdom. And the 'feeble' things of God have proven to be far more powerful than any human ability" (1 Corinthians 1:25).

LET'S PRAY

Almighty God, I'm humbled as I come before you today. I bow in reverence and awe of you. Your ways are so much higher than mine. Give me a passion for pursuing you and your plan for my life. Give me grace for steps of obedience that will bring your favor upon me. I long to know and to complete your divine will for my life. I surrender to you today, in Jesus' name. Amen.

6

FAITH AND PATIENCE

Our "heavenly Joshua" is more than enough to empower us to overcome every stronghold. There is never a lack of power available for your life. What releases the powerful life of Jesus into us? Faith. But you say, "Why am I not seeing more victory? I have faith in his promises. I have faith in his power to fill me and use." Yes, but do you have patience?

> Don't allow your hearts to grow dull or lose your
> enthusiasm, but follow the example of those who
> fully received what God has promised because
> of their strong faith and patient endurance.
> (Hebrews 6:12)

In other words, don't be disappointed by the process, for the Scripture verse says that it's by faith and patient endurance that we inherit the promises. The word *dull* is taken from a root word meaning "illegitimate child." The implication is that we must not see ourselves as a child of illegitimacy but as a child of intimacy. We are God's beloved children and must keep our relationship with him fervent and passionate, even if it seems our progress is slow. Now we're ready for the next strategic key for the Joshua generation.

KEY #5: A LITTLE AT A TIME

Upon our salvation, we've received every blessing heaven contains in Jesus Christ. Yet, there's still a growth process that we all must go through. It takes time to mature into the fullness of Christ's likeness. Because the process seems to be prolonged, some grow dull—feeling like Father God has forgotten them— rather than understanding the preparation process that we all must experience.

Don't let the process rob you of joy! Keep on going for him no matter how you feel. Encourage yourself in the Lord and press in for more. You must remain hungry for more. Hunger for what you see in the lives of other Christians around you who have been serving him for years. If you are faithful, you will soon get there. Each breakthrough will prepare you for the next.

For forty years, Israel wandered and rejected the process of growing in faith and patient endurance. For that reason, they could not enter into their inheritance. Now, a new generation rises, a Joshua generation, and they must not repeat the failures of a previous generation. Remain faithful, my friend, no matter how long the process. Jesus is worth it all!

God has a part, and we have our part. We can't do his part, and he won't do ours. We must embrace his wonderful promises and step out in faith. For instance, here's a wonderful promise given to Joshua, which I believe we can take for ourselves: "Every part of the land where you march, I will give you, as I promised Moses" (Joshua 1:3).

He'll give you every place that you set your foot upon. How powerful it is when we choose to partner with the God of the Universe. For nothing is impossible with him, and likewise, nothing is impossible for you as you go forward at his command. Faith will demolish your strongholds; it is the victory that overcomes the world! Stepping out with more faith equals possessing more of your inheritance. The promises God has given you for your family, your finances, and your future depend upon your faith to activate them. Step out and claim them today.

KEY #6: YOU MUST BE STRONG

"Be strong and brave" were the words Joshua heard God himself speak to him. This generation needs to hear this. We all need to hear it. Be strong, don't give up, and don't worry about momentary problems. It'll be alright. It'll work out, and you'll be okay. So be strong and brave!

> You must be strong and brave. (Joshua 1:6)

> I repeat, be strong and brave! Do not yield to fear
> nor be discouraged, for I am YAHWEH your God,
> and I will be with you wherever you go! (Joshua 1:9)

Joshua was facing a lot of handicaps. He basically took a youth group into the promised land to fight against giants. Can you imagine? They had no weapons or military experience, and the walls of the city were high. But God kept telling them to be strong and courageous. All they had was God, and he is always more than enough. He is a majority. So, don't worry. You, too, have God and his strength. The Almighty has this, and so do you. Almighty and family!

There are unique tasks that this generation must rise to. The Joshua generation of this era must go in and topple those strongholds that Moses couldn't. Moses didn't knock down Jericho's walls, but Joshua and his followers did. We must be strong where others may have failed to finish.

Not only do we need to listen to the preceding generation, but there are things that only the Holy Spirit can teach us. And if we have good mentors, they'll teach us to hear the Holy Spirit for ourselves because the Holy Spirit will take us further than any man can. True spiritual enlightenment and revelation are the specialties of the Holy Spirit. Men can open a door for us, but we must go past them to fulfill what God has for us. Only then can we complete our mission for our own generation.

LET'S PRAY

Lord, sometimes I feel so weak. I know that I could never enter into your fullness without your strength. I lay my weakness before you. I exchange my weakness for your strength. I want to rise and not fall. I want to do exploits for you and your kingdom. Empower me today with strength and might in my inner being. I trust in you alone, my Lord and my God. Amen.

7

BOLDNESS

KEY #7: BE BOLD

Please don't forget this. No one will be able to defeat you all the days of your life. Hear the voice of the Lord saying to you today, *Be strong...be bold and courageous!* You don't have to go with the crowd. The crowds have never gone with God anyway. They have no idea. True courage is in those who find their strength in the secret place of the Most High. They find those pathways that fallen people have never seen before, the place that the falcon's eye has never seen, nor has the eagle ever flown (see Job 28:7). They find the discerning way. God said to Joshua,

> No one will be able to defeat you for the rest of your life! I will be with you as I was with Moses, and I will never fail nor abandon you. (Joshua 1:5)

If you ask me, this is the greatest encouragement any of us could possibly receive. Can you imagine how Joshua must have felt? We all do better when we're affirmed by the support of others. And in this case, this was not just another; this was God! God was basically saying to him, *Moses is dead, but you know what, Joshua? Just as you saw me work miracles through your amazing leader, I'm going to be with you in the same way. I'm going to work and flow through you. I'm going to show you my life the way I showed Moses. And I'm going to speak to you.* Then just two chapters later, God appears to Joshua with his sword drawn. The Commander of Angel Armies actually manifests in person to him. He *was* with Joshua all the way. And in the same way God was with Joshua, God is also with you. Enter in today and find him to be more than enough.

Bury the Past to Seize the New Day Ahead

Can you just imagine if a whole generation sat there for forty years and just mourned over and over, saying, "Where's Moses? How can we go on without Moses? Where's the guy who opened the rock up so that water gushed out for us?" No. God has a new generation with a new destiny and a new calling. A new breed of leaders is rising. So, seize it! Seize the mantle of the Joshua generation. Rise up and take it. It's yours! But if you don't, somebody else will. Grab it and run with the torch and run with the vision. Do you know what keeps you from doing it? It's called the fear of failure. But God in you will never fail you or leave you! In him you are more than a conqueror! Remember what God said to Joshua: "Be strong and courageous!"

You've just got to be who you are. Joshua had been trained by Moses, but he wasn't Moses. Moses laid his hands on him and anointed him, but still he wasn't Moses. Can you imagine the people saying to Joshua, "Oh, but you're not Moses. We want Moses. Who do you think you are? You were only his assistant. You were just the junior guy. Your gifts are so different, and your personality is different than Moses'. And where's the rod? You're not carrying a rod." You can imagine the insecurity that may have been working against Joshua. Every budding leader goes through that. But we must rise up and walk in our own anointing.

You don't have the problems Joshua did, like taking a youth group into the promised land. Your problems are different, but you have the same God. Joshua didn't even have a weapon, and there were walled cities and giants. Joshua had a lot to face ahead of him, but God said to him, like he's saying to you, "Don't worry. You will go in my strength against the enemies for I am God Almighty." God's got this, and he's got you.

Be strong and brave. It's the few who find him in the secret place, and that's where they find their strength. Jesus walked on water. And so, the ways of those who follow after him will also find the paths that have never been mapped out. They will find the hidden path to the hidden place of God's heart. They will be strong and brave and change the world. "For I am YAHWEH your God, and I will be with you wherever you go" (Joshua 1:9).

LET'S PRAY

God, I ask for boldness. At times, I have struggled with passivity. I've chosen an easy path instead of the ways of self-discipline and walking in supernatural boldness. I repent and ask you again, give me courage. Make me a part of the Joshua generation that will not shrink back in a time of trouble, but one who will race to face my giants, as did David. I want the boldness that the blood of Jesus has purchased for me. I want the boldness that only your Holy Spirit can give me. And ask you to do in my life today. Amen.

8

A Time to Conquer

Joshua is the book of conquest. It takes us from theory into the reality of possessing our inheritance. This is the apostolic, city-reaching manual for the last days. There is new territory to possess; the Hebrew word *land* is found eighty-seven times in Joshua alone. There are cities that must be reached and enemies to be dislodged from power. It will require a new breed of bold, fearless deliverers to move the church forward in this hour.

Three times in verses 1–9 the Lord tells Joshua to be strong and brave. We need strength and courage today as never before. You will face enemies and walled cities that look impossible to conquer. Armies will stand in front of you, taunting you and your faith. But remain strong, bold, and courageous. One leader with courage makes a majority!

The first thing God did to prepare a million people to cross over into their inheritance was to encourage their leader. Most leaders don't need advice as much as they need encouragement. They need the strength of God to advance. But where does our strength come from? The divine source of our strength is the life of Jesus Christ within us. The promises of God, Jesus living within us, and the Holy Spirit will be more than enough.

> The strength of Christ's explosive power infuses me to conquer every difficulty. (Philippians 4:13)

> Lord, so many times I fail; I fall into disgrace. But when I trust in you, I have a strong and glorious presence protecting and anointing me. Forever you're all I need! (Psalm 73:26)

THE WORD OF GOD IS OUR WEAPON

God commissioned Joshua to achieve three things: lead the people into the land, defeat the enemy, and claim the inheritance. God could have sent an angel to do this, but he chose to use a man and to give him the power he needed to get the job done. As we have already seen, Joshua is a type of Jesus Christ, the pioneer of our salvation (see Hebrews 2:10), who has won the victory and now shares his spiritual inheritance with us.

God also gave three promises in Joshua's great commission: they would cross over the Jordan, they would take cities, and they would divide the inheritance. And God gave Joshua three commands: you must possess what I have given you, be strong and courageous, and always keep the Word of God central in your heart.

> Recite this scroll of the law constantly. Contemplate it[3] day and night and be careful to follow every

word it contains; then you will enjoy incredible
prosperity and success. (Joshua 1:8)

Success and incredible prosperity would come to Joshua if
he made the words of God the most important thing in his life.
He was to recite them constantly, speaking them over his life, his
family, and the battles he would face. It is impossible to calculate
how many lives have been changed forever by the power of the
Bible, the living Word of God. My life was transformed forever
because I believed the message contained in the Scriptures about
Jesus, the Savior. Whether it's a Scripture website, a phone app, or
a book in your hand, the message of God's love and power shines
brightly on every page. The Bible is our eternal standard and the
foundation of our faith. The Bible is important. It matters that we
believe it. The Bible is the throbbing heart of our faith. Tear out
that heart, and our belief system is dead. Every follower of Jesus
shares a belief system deeply rooted in the Bible. Believers from
every age and every culture have a standard, the gold standard of
our faith—our amazing Bible! The importance of the Scriptures
cannot be overstated.

The Scriptures are important because they tell us all we need
to know about Jesus. He is our hero and human model. He means
more to us than any person. He gave his life for us (see 1 Timothy
2:3–6). Although we have never seen him, we love him and
long for the day when we will see him face-to-face. Without the
Scriptures, we would know almost nothing about Jesus. It is the
Bible that gives us detailed information about who Jesus is, why he
was born, why he died, how he rose again, and where he went after
his ascension. He is the Bible's greatest hero, the mighty God-Man
who conquers evil and comes to our rescue.

Every day as I read the Bible, I look for Jesus. He is there on every page, including in the book of Joshua. His living presence is with me as I read and discover more of who he is. This quest to find Jesus in the Word has been rewarded over and over by seeing more of him. He lives in the letters of Paul, the gospels, the history of Israel, creation's glory, and the consummation of the ages. Jesus is the Teacher of my heart and the Shepherd of my soul. Your great delight will be to find him in your daily Bible reading.

Everything we need for life and godliness is found in the written Scriptures. I'm thrilled to see how the Word changes lives. We saw it in our jungle village when the Paya-Kuna had the completed New Testament, and we have seen it today as millions of lives are being transformed by its living truth.

The Word of God and the Holy Spirit are married. The Spirit is the divine spouse of the Word. They will never separate or file for divorce. You cannot have one without the other. Those who are part of the Joshua generation will not only have the power and gifts of the Holy Spirit, but they will also have the revelation of the Word of God burning in their hearts.

LET'S PRAY

Jesus, you are all I need. Whatever I face today, your strength and your promises will see me through. You have won so many victories in my life. You have subdued my wayward soul and caused my heart to burn with holy desires to please you. Take my life today and use me to glorify your name and display your power. In your holy name I pray. Amen.

9

Confident Faith

I once heard a true story of a British preacher who sailed to America over a hundred years ago. He was an anointed and godly man. God had spoken to him and told him to come to America. The problem was that it would take him about two weeks on a steamship, which was an expensive trip for his meager income. He barely had enough money, but he saved and borrowed money from his family to scrape together enough to pay for the price of the ticket.

The story goes that as he was getting on the ship, his mother came and handed him a brown paper bag of food saying, "It's going to be a long trip. You're going to need something to eat." And he was so thankful for the food that she had put together for him in that humble, brown paper bag. Every day during his almost two weeks of crossing the Atlantic, he would walk by the opulent dining room where the wealthy were eating and enjoying their feasts. Then he would go back to his tiny little corner of the ship, where he would eat some of the crackers and smoked fish his mother had packed for him. Then the day came when his food finally ran out, and he had nothing else to eat.

Day after day after day, he would pass by and see all the people enjoying themselves and living the good life while he was so hungry. At the end of the two weeks, when they were finally nearing New York, he happened to overhear some people talking about the meals they enjoyed on board. They remarked on how wonderful all the food had been. And they were so glad that all of it had been included in the price of the ticket. What? He had been eating crumbs when all the food he would ever need had already been provided.

How many of us are "brown paper bagging it" in our life when the whole package of salvation has already provided everything we need? Everything you want in Jesus Christ is yours already! You can't have any more than you already have. It's impossible. The Father has blessed you with every spiritual blessing in Christ (see Ephesians 1:3). The book of Joshua is a clear picture of our spiritual inheritance that we have in Christ right now.

This should be our faith confession: *I've already won every victory in Christ. I've already won every spiritual battle that I will ever face because I'm in Christ.* You see, faith is the victory that overcomes the world. Faith brings us victory in every situation. We may think that we need more strength, more tools, more education, more friends, or more connections. But we need to realize that faith in God alone is the way to victory. We don't just need permission or more power; we need faith.

SPIES SENT TO JERICHO

This is what the Lord would want to teach us today: we have already won every single battle. Joshua believed it and took God at his word. Strategically, he sent two spies into Jericho in Canaan just as God's people were getting ready to cross over the flooding river of Jordan to enter the promised land. He was confident of their victory because God had already promised him, but they still had the work of partnering with God to see it done. Moses sent twelve spies; Joshua only sent two. Moses sent his spies because of the unbelief of the people, but Joshua sent two spies because of the faith that filled his heart. He wanted them to come back and bring to the people the verbal proof that God had indeed already gone ahead of them.

When the spies entered Jericho, they ended up at the house of Rahab, the harlot's house. And when the king of Jericho discovered that the spies had arrived in his city, he searched for them. He was informed that they had gone into Rahab's house. You see, by faith, she risked herself and her family's lives to hide them. Rahab had heard the news of all the miracles that God had accomplished for the people of Israel. Faith was rising in her heart to believe that this God, YAHWEH, was the true God. She became the first convert in Canaan.

When the king's men arrived at her house, she quickly hid Joshua's spies on the housetop under flax (see Joshua 2:6).[4] Rahab misled the king's soldiers and told them that the Hebrew spies had gone out of the city, and she sent them looking in the wrong direction. Then she directed the spies safely out of the city, telling them how to escape.

The two spies eventually made it back to their base camp and gave Joshua a powerful report. They told him that the inhabitants of Jericho were trembling in their boots and that the people of Jericho realized that the God of Heaven and Earth was among them and coming to the aid of the Israelites. God would provide all that they needed, even a miracle!

So, don't "brown paper bag it" when God has gone ahead of you to fight your battles. His wraparound glory will be more than enough for you.

LET'S PRAY

Father, everything about you satisfies my soul. You have provided all that I have needed, for great is your faithfulness. Today, I want the faith to believe that every need and every challenge is already met by the fullness of Christ in me. You have given me all things for life and godly living. I draw your strength into my need today as I pray in faith. Amen.

10

A Covenant of Hope

"Please solemnly swear to me by the name of YAHWEH that you will show kindness to my family because I have shown kindness to you. Give me a sure sign that you will spare the lives of my father and mother, my brothers and sisters, and all their families. Don't let us be killed!"

JOSHUA 2:12–13

Oh, what a woman Rahab was! Before she sent the spies away, she wanted a sign that she and her precious family would be saved. There's nothing in the passage that says her family believed in God like she did. But she cared about her family even though they were likely outside of the covenant of God. She had to go out and convince them to come into her house when the Hebrews came to destroy their city. You can imagine the intense discussions Rahab had with her loved ones. There is no doubt about it;

Rahab's compassion-filled faith surely changed her world and her family's world.

Rahab's faith was a covenant faith. This covenant faith was shown in that she had made an agreement, a contract. She understood the oath and believed that the spies were telling the truth. She believed that God himself would protect them.

> The men answered, "If you don't disclose our mission to anyone, we'll pledge our lives for yours. Then, when YAHWEH gives us this land, we'll honor our promise and treat you kindly."…
>
> But the men warned her, "You must do what we say, or we will not be bound to the oath you made us swear. When our invasion begins, bring all your family together in your house—your father and mother, your brothers, sisters, and all their families. And tie this crimson rope in the same window through which you let us down. Remember, if anyone ventures outside your house, his death will be his own fault, not ours! But if anyone inside your house is harmed, then we will be held responsible. And if you disclose our mission, we will be released from the oath you made us swear."
>
> Rahab replied in agreement, "Let it be as you say." And she sent them away, and after they departed, she tied the crimson rope in her window. (Joshua 2:14, 17–21)

Our God is a covenant-making God. He wants to partner with us. He is looking for those with whom he can come into agreement, like Abraham, Moses, David, and, as we see here, Rahab. And Rahab, being in covenant faith with God through the spies, puts this scarlet rope in her window. It was not a scarlet cord or thread, as I've read in some versions. No, this is a rope. This is a big rope you could climb up or down on. She put a scarlet rope out to signify she believed in the covenant. The Passover blood of the Lamb was scarlet and sprinkled on the doorposts. Rahab had a "blood-stained" rope, as it were, a scarlet rope hanging in her window as a sign and testimony that she believed in God.

The Hebrew word for "rope" is *tikvah,* a homonym for *hope.* Yes, the Hebrew word for hope is the same word for Rahab's rope. It's the rope of hope! What do a rope and hope have in common? A rope is formed by entwining multiple strands into one cord. So hope is more than passive waiting; it is entwining our hearts into God's heart. Hope is a rope that we can hang on to when the world seems out of control or when we don't know how to make it through a difficult season in life. God has wonderful plans for you, to give you a future and a hope (*tikvah*) (see Jeremiah 29:11).

The men said to Rahab that this oath would not be binding unless she tied the scarlet rope in the window. Rahab had faith in the Lord and in the covenant promises he had made. She proved her faith by hanging the scarlet rope from the window. When the Hebrews captured Jericho, they found Rahab and her family in her house, and they rescued them from judgment. Rahab was a woman of great courage and covenant. We will talk more about Rahab in a later chapter.

Rahab took the Hebrew spies into her home knowing that it could cost her life. She was the only person in Jericho who trusted the God of Israel, and so God brought the spies to her. It's remarkable how God uses people like prostitutes and preachers, carpenters and office people, accountants, realtors, mothers, artists, teachers, and you! God has chosen the foolish things. He is talking about us.

> God chose those whom the world considers foolish to shame those who think they are wise, and God chose the puny and powerless to shame the high and mighty. He chose the lowly, the laughable in the world's eyes—nobodies—so that he would shame the somebodies. For he chose what is regarded as insignificant in order to supersede what is regarded as prominent, so that there would be no place for prideful boasting in God's presence. (1 Corinthians 1: 27–29)

Some of the boldest, most competent, most courageous warriors of God are women. Anointed women are rising. They're rising fully anointed and courageous. They're moving forward because the gifts of God are in them. They have the anointing, the authority, the boldness, and the same gifts that men have. The Joshua generation will have powerful leaders who are both men and women. So together, we will step into our destiny, women and men together. Faith is our victory, and it doesn't matter where you've been or what you have been through. Like Rahab, God will use your story for his glory. Let your faith arise! Remember, when you step out in courageous, confident, compassionate faith that moves in covenant with God, lives will be changed, mountains will move, and walls will fall.

Let's Pray

I need you today, Holy Spirit. Come and fill me with your power and grace. I confess my need for you. I must have you flowing in my life, or I will fail. Your sweet presence sustains me and gives me endless hope. Flood into my inner being until I am filled and overflow with your fruit and wisdom. I trust you, Holy Spirit. Amen.

I I

PREPARING TO CROSS OVER

What an incredible picture of faith we see in this true story of
the book of Joshua. Think with me about what the situation was
like for Joshua and the children of Israel. It was truly a moment
of moments for them. They had to cross the Jordan River, yet it
was almost a mile wide at flood stage.[5] They had no boat, no rope,
no bridge. And to make matters worse, there were fortified cities
standing in front of them, and giants were in the land. They didn't
have weapons, they weren't a trained army, and they were just coming out of a long journey of wilderness wanderings. Everything in
front of them was insurmountable. Everything looked hopeless
and screamed, "Impossible!" The only thing they really had going
for them was God. It was God plus nothing. God alone. And they
found that the All-Sufficient One was all they needed!

For three days, Joshua and the people stared at the flooding river that separated them from their inheritance. How was God going to pull it off? There was no possible way they could cross the flood without drowning. Why did God make them wait three days? Because amazing things happen on the third day! The third day is the day of resurrection power. Jesus was raised from the cold, dark tomb on the third day. God wanted his people to understand that it would take resurrection power for them to cross into their inheritance. And so, for us today, God's mighty power is required to break death off our lives and break us loose from the shame and guilt of our wilderness wanderings.

LET'S GO!

Joshua was up bright and early the next morning. They broke camp, and Joshua led the Israelites from Acacia to the eastern bank of the Jordan. There they set up camp and waited until they crossed over. After three days, the leaders of the people went throughout the camp giving orders to the people, "Watch for the priests of the tribe of Levi to lift the ark of the covenant of YAHWEH[6] your God. When it starts moving, follow it so you'll know which way to go, since you've never marched this way before.[7] Follow about a half mile behind the ark; don't go near it."

Joshua instructed the people, "Get yourselves ready! Set yourselves apart for YAHWEH! Tomorrow, YAHWEH will perform for us great miracles!"[8]

> Joshua told the priests, "Raise up the ark of the covenant and step out ahead of the people." So they lifted the ark onto their shoulders and marched in front of the people. (Joshua 3:1–6)

When the three days of their preparation and self-emptying had finished, they broke camp and made the nearly eight-mile hike for the Jordan. What an exciting day this was for Joshua and the people! They were about to leave their wandering in the wilderness behind. A new beginning was now before them. All but two men were under forty years old and had been born in the desert; now they would cross over into a fertile land. Anticipation was in the air. After three days of waiting near a flooding river, they were about to see a miracle.

The people were to keep their eyes on the ark of glory and follow it. The priests would carry the ark (symbolic of God's presence) on their shoulders a half mile ahead of them. As they descended the valley to the riverbank, everyone would be able to see the ark and the miracle for themselves.

The Joshua generation will not be distracted from nor disrespectful of the glory of God. They will set their hearts on following God's presence. In the wilderness, the Israelites followed the cloud of glory; now they are to follow the ark of glory. God has different ways of leading his people. And true wisdom will let God choose the best path ahead.

The miracle of the Jordan crossing would prepare a million people to enter a land of giants, obstacles, and walled cities. They needed the preparation of seeing this miracle before they took the land. Get ready; a season of miracles is ahead for you. There will be bumps along the way and battles to face, but our God will be more than enough.

LET'S PRAY

King of Glory, my eyes are on you. I purpose in my heart not to be moved or distracted by the difficulties of this day. I know that you are with me, my Shepherd and my King. Lead the way. Show me the right path. Work a miracle in my life and my family today. Amen.

12

GETTING YOUR FEET WET

YAHWEH said to Joshua, "This very day I will begin to exalt you in the sight of all Israel so that they will realize that I am with you in the same way I was with Moses. You are to command the priests who carry the ark of the covenant with these words: 'Carry the ark to the edge of the Jordan and wade into the water.'"

JOSHUA 3:7–8

A miracle requires that you step out in faith and get your feet wet. Peter did. He stepped out of the boat, the confining "box" in which he lived, and he stood on top of the water (see Matthew 14:22–33). Faith will empower you to stand on top of your limitation. Now it was time for a miracle for the Israelites. But the miracle required that the priests wade into the water.

Joshua told the Israelites, "Come closer and listen to the words of YAHWEH your God. This is how you

55

will know for sure that the Living God is among you. As you advance into the land, he will drive out before you the Canaanites, Hittites, Hivites, Perizzites, Girgashites, Amorites, and Jebusites. Look! The ark of the covenant of the Lord of all the earth will go before you and prepare a way for you through the Jordan. (Joshua 3:9–11)

God promised an overwhelming victory to the people of Israel. But they had to advance. They could not hold back or linger in complacency. Keep advancing, my friend! Don't stop! A passive spirit will not be a part of the Joshua generation. They will not hold back but will be like horses charging into the battle, ready to see the triumph of God (see Joel 2:4–5).

"The moment the feet of the priests carrying the ark of YAHWEH, the Lord of all the earth, touch the water of the Jordan, a great miracle will happen! The water flowing downstream toward you will stop and pile up as if behind a dam."

Now it was time for the early harvest, and the river was overflowing at flood stage. When the people broke camp to cross the Jordan, the priests went in front of them carrying the ark of the covenant on their shoulders. The very moment the priests with the ark dipped their feet in the river's edge, the water coming downstream stopped flowing and piled up in a solid wall as far upstream as Adam, a place near Zarethan. YAHWEH completely cut off the flow of the river so that it drained downstream toward the Desert Sea (the

Dead Sea). So the people crossed over opposite Jericho. (Joshua 3:13–16)

See what "getting your feet wet" will do? What a sight! At the very moment the toes of the priest touched the river water, a miracle happened. The river split in two. Half rolled upstream, and the other half raced downstream to the Dead Sea, leaving only dry ground for the people to cross over. What made this miracle even greater was that the river Jordan was flooding. This was not a little stream you could jump over. Folks, it was over a half mile wide! Our God is mighty!

A Miracle near a Town Called Adam

The miracle-crossing of the Jordan River stands as one of the greatest miracles of the Bible. God split the Red Sea, he split open a rock so a river would flow out to quench the thirst of his people, and now he parts the Jordan River with his ark of glory. The waters were held back and formed a lake that would have extended for many miles. Who says God cannot work a miracle for you and break every limitation off your destiny? If God has sent you, he will move heaven and earth and water to make you succeed.

So, the water upstream piled high seventeen miles away at a town called "Adam." Let's connect the dots. The river Jordan represents the death of Jesus on the cross and the price he paid to save us. The word for "Jordan" is a Hebrew compound word, joining the words for "to descend" and "judging" (judgment). Jesus, our Ark of Glory, descended into judgment for our sins and rolled the river of guilt, shame, and judgment all the way back to Adam! The sin of humanity was rolled away by one Man, Jesus Christ. But there was another town nearby, a town called Zarethan. The root word for *Zarethan* is a verb that means "piercing" or "bleeding of the veins." Judgment was abated to Adam's family by the one who was "pierced" for our rebellious deeds. He bled to death to have you. Will you give your heart today to the one who would rather suffer and die for you than live in heaven without you?

LET'S PRAY

God, I'm humbled as I come before you. My life, my strength, and my hope are in you alone. I owe my life to you, my breath, my thoughts, my joys. I give them all to you in gratitude for all you have done for me. I'm overwhelmed by your grace. Take my life today and make me an example of what eternal life can really look like here on earth. Win my battles and be glorified in me. Amen.

13

CROSSING OVER

Now the priests stood firmly on dry ground in the riverbed with the ark on their shoulders. The entire nation passed by the ark as they completed their miracle-crossing on dry ground.[9]

JOSHUA 3:17

I wish I could have been there! What a sight as the river parted and the once muddy riverbed became dry ground. A wide path opened for the people to cross over. The priests stood in the middle of the riverbed, and every single person walked right by the ark of glory. Only the high priests could come into the Holy of Holies where the ark stood, but now the entire nation gets to walk by it with their jaws dropped open! The waters of death and judgment stopped flowing when Jesus was crucified. Now, when we believe, the waters of life and glory cascade into us.

Our old Adam-life was buried figuratively at the place Israel crossed into their inheritance. It was like a death, burial, and resurrection for a million people crossing over on dry ground after a three-day wait. So, too, have we crossed over into resurrection life with Jesus to possess our inheritance as a people delivered and redeemed.

> Have you forgotten that all of us who were immersed into union with Jesus Christ, the Anointed One, were immersed into union with his death?
>
> Sharing in his death by our baptism means that we were co-buried, so that when the Father's glory raised Christ from the dead, we were also raised with him. We have been co-resurrected with him so that we could be empowered to walk in the freshness of new life. (Romans 6:3–4)

THE PRIESTS CARRY THE ARK

There stood the priests on dry ground, waiting for a million people to cross. It would have taken the greater part of one day for all the men carrying their possessions and the women carrying their young to cross over. They stood for many hours with the heavy ark on their shoulders. What a test of faithful endurance. Yet we are also called to be his faithful "priests" (see 1 Peter 2:9; Revelation 5:9–10). Made holy by Lamb's blood, we are priests who stand on the dry ground of the finished work of Christ.

Do you realize that God wouldn't have gone into the river and worked a miracle if someone hadn't carried him? It was God on human legs (in this case, it would have been eight legs, four men) carrying the ark. God and man stood in the water together as a picture of the Lord Jesus, who is fully God and fully man. All that God wants to accomplish in your destiny happens with both you and God united. If you leave out God and think you're going to accomplish it alone, it's not going to happen. If you think it's going to be God without your yielded "yes," it won't happen. It is true that everything we do is only by his grace and mercy, but even so, God is not going to come down and do what he has already commanded and empowered you and me to do. He won't come down and pray for you. Nor will he come down to feed the poor and needy. He's not going to come down and serve your community. You are! You're going to do it with God's grace. We don't want to receive God's grace in vain. We are coworkers with God. It is a divine partnership, a divine duet.

So many of the blessings of God come upon our life, but if we do nothing with them, then it's all in vain. We may be anointed. We may have great favor. We may get mercy, a spiritual gift, or advancement in some area of our life, but then we must use that which we've been given. We must implement it and apply the blessings of God in every aspect of our lives, or we waste those blessings.

As long as God and man work together, it's good. As long as you and God are in holy tandem in this divine partnership, you're going to succeed, advance, and possess your inheritance. However, as soon as you start fretting over whether God is going to do his part, you've missed the point. Believe me, God has never been unfaithful. He's never failed you. He never will. He'll never abandon you. He'll never leave you "half done." He'll never start something and not finish well. We're the ones who need to identify ourselves with the zeal of the Lord. We need to press ourselves into the very burning heart of God until we become one with him.

The book of Joshua teaches us how God and his people unite and work together. Two become one, God and his people. He wants to unite us to his purpose. YAHWEH's plan is and always has been that we would unite our hearts to him and take our land (move into our destiny) together. The great mystery, the gateway to fascination, is when man yields to God and God yields to man. It's where God lets man bring him into the promise. Listen, God will yield to the prayer of a man, and man will yield to the call of God. This is truly the gateway to fascination. This is divine mystery. This holy place of life-union and communion between God and man is a threshold of the supernatural realm. It's the mystery of the bride, the bride of Christ.

LET'S PRAY

> God of Glory, I bow before you in wonder and awe of the mysteries of heaven. I know so little. I have your fullness, yet I live in only a portion of the immense treasure that I have in Christ. Release in me greater measures of that fullness. Open the eyes of my understanding until I comprehend the vast measure of what you have given me in the Lord Jesus Christ, my Savior. I want it all. In your holy name, amen.

14

THE ARK

While the priests remained standing in the middle of the Jordan with the ark on their shoulders, the people hurried across. All the instructions YAHWEH had given to Joshua were carried out—just as Moses had told Joshua. And when Israel had finished crossing, the ark of YAHWEH and the priests crossed as the people looked on.

JOSHUA 4:10–11

Man must bring God into the land. The ark of glory was carried across the Jordan on the shoulders of the priests. The shoulders speak of the place of authority, for Scripture says in Isaiah 9:6 that "the government shall be upon his shoulder" (KJV). In the same way, we usher in the government of God to the earth with authority and strength. However, man must submit this strength to God. The glory of God wants to come upon your shoulders. You don't need to worry about being too weak. There's nobody reading this who is too weak for God. Blessed are the weak, and blessed are the poor, for they will walk into the inheritance of God's kingdom (see Matthew 5:3–12). Weakness isn't our problem, but rather our strength is. It's our strengths that God will subdue: our cleverness, our brilliance, our solutions to every problem. It's the strategy that's born out of clever scheming and striving that causes us problems. It's the strength of human nature that so often gets in the way of God. It's Jacob's thigh that has yet to be knocked out of joint. So, it's the shoulder of man where God's glory must rest to subdue and cover us.

Man must bring God into the land, and God must bring man into his inheritance. How did man bring God in? By carrying him on his shoulders. How did God bring man in? By parting the waters. Hallelujah! The Hebrews had nothing to fear as long as they were partnering with God. You have nothing to fear if you partner with him. If you walk in passivity and wait and wait and wait instead of stepping out into the fullness of his plans, you will miss something God has in store for you. You will miss your inheritance.

As Christians we must become spiritually aggressive. We need to inspire and motivate the bride of Christ to rise up and come away. And it must become the personal goal of every Christian to respond to God's call. It's time to step out and step into the purpose that God has called you to. Your destiny is to possess all that Calvary-love has purchased for you. You will never reach the realm of abundant living if you remain where you are. You'll never get there by simply hoping and wishing. So many of us are great at making plans. We've got high hopes and wishes. We have our fantasies, and we have our ideas and our visions for how we want our lives to go. However, the best plan in the world will never take place until you step out into the undiscovered country of faith-filled living. You must get out of your comfort zone and into the zone where you can't always predict what's coming. It is the place of divine partnership. And, oh, what a powerful place that is! The unpredictable God will step in with his predictable goodness and show you the way. The Joshua generation is made for living in the fullness that Christ has purchased for us!

STEP INTO THE CO-CRUCIFIED LIFE

Every person went into the river, and every person crossed to the other side. It wasn't just the ark-carrying priests. It was every one of God's people. They all had to go through to the other side. They all entered the Jordan, representing death and judgment. Let me say it clearly: one nail, two hands. One nail went through two hands, yours and Jesus'. Your hand and Jesus' hand were crucified together. We are co-crucified with Christ. We died with Jesus Christ. This is the Gospel for Christians: you have been crucified with Christ. You don't have to try not to sin anymore. "Come and let Christ live his life through you." The Gospel for sinners is, "Come to Christ and be saved."

You must realize that you entered into the waters of death, into the Jordan experience of crossing over. In doing so, you became one with Christ in crucifixion. He died *for my sins*. I died *to my sin*. He died so that I would not face the *judgment of sin*. I died so that I would not have to face the *power of sin*. I am and can be set free forever. I've entered death, and dead people don't sin. There is no sin in a graveyard (unless living people get in there somehow!), and you are likewise dead to sin. Isn't that powerful?

CO-BURIED

Not only did we die with him, but we were also buried with him. Let the truth of that sink in. You see, the waters of judgment washed over Christ, and they washed over us, and we, too, were put in the tomb. One tomb, two people. We were co-buried. We're not only co-crucified with Christ, but we also went into the Jordan River. The ark of covenant took us there. The waters of judgment rolled back, but our old nature, our Adam-life, stayed right there buried under the water forever.

CO-RAISED

Thank God we crossed over into resurrection ground. We were not only co-crucified, we were not only co-buried, but we were also co-raised with him. We were lifted on high. We got to go on the other side of the Jordan. Can you imagine a million people being united with the ark of glory in the Jordan River and then going onto the other side and being raised to newness of life? One nail, two hands, one tomb, two people. One stone rolled away, and we were raised to newness of life.

CO-SEATED

Okay, let's go over this again: co-crucified, co-buried, co-raised...but it gets even better! We are also co-seated with Christ. We are co-raised but not just six feet off the ground. We are raised up to the very heavens! We're sitting in the heavenly places in Christ. Nothing evil is going to get to you. Your life is hidden with Christ in God. I've read Colossians 3, and I believe it. I've been seated with Christ in heavenly places, and so have you. As Ephesians 2:6 says, we've been raised up together with him and seated together with him. One throne...two people!

COHEIR

Now it gets *even* better. Not only were we co-crucified, co-buried, co-raised, and co-seated, but we are coheirs. You and I are joint heirs of all things, co-inheritors and co-signers to the title deed of the universe. Everything Jesus does requires our signature. And just when you thought it couldn't get any better, there's more!

CO-LABORER

We're also co-laborers with Christ. The anointing of Jesus and his favor are on my life. Wherever I go, he goes with me. We have a divine partnership. We have a contract, and I've signed my rights over. Wherever he leads, I follow. We can go into the cities and nations of the earth, bold and fearless. Why? Because we're co-laborers, partners together with Jesus. Eternity's partnership has taken place. We have crossed over into the land of our inheritance.

LET'S PRAY

Father God, how can I thank you for all you have done for me? Your precious gift of eternal life is my hope and my joy. I bless you, thank you, and praise you for endless ages. I love you, Jesus. I am blessed beyond measure because of your love for me. Your blood is my eternal hope. Your Spirit is my strength. Thank you for the co-union we share. Amen.

15

TWELVE STONES

When the entire nation had finished their miracle-crossing of the Jordan, YAHWEH said to Joshua, "Choose twelve men, one from each of the twelve tribes of Israel. Instruct each of them to take a stone from the riverbed, twelve stones from the very place where the priests stand with the ark. Have them carry the stones over to the place where you camp tonight."

So Joshua summoned the twelve men he had selected from the Israelites, one per tribe. Joshua instructed them, "Walk out to the middle of the riverbed to the ark of YAHWEH your God. Each of you choose a stone and lift it up onto your shoulder—one stone for each tribe. The stones will always be a sign to you. Someday, when your children ask you, 'Why are these stones so important?' tell them, 'The Jordan stopped flowing in front of the ark of the covenant of YAHWEH—the floodwaters were completely cut off.' These stones will serve as a memorial for Israel forever."

The Israelites did as Joshua commanded them. They took twelve stones according to the number of tribes of Israel, from the middle of the riverbed, and carried them to the camp and put them there. Joshua set up the memorial stones that they had taken from the exact spot where the priests stood bearing the ark in the riverbed. They remain there to this day.
While the priest remained standing in the middle of the Jordan with the ark on their shoulders, the people hurried across...
The Reubenites, the Gadites, and the half tribe of Manasseh went across, armed and ready for battle, in front of the Israelites...And they all marched before YAHWEH to wage war on the plains of Jericho.

JOSHUA 4:1–10, 12–13

A MEMORIAL TO IMPOSSIBILITIES

After crossing, the people went up from the Jordan, and they camped at Gilgal on the eastern border of Jericho. Joshua then set up at Gilgal the twelve stones that they had taken up out of the Jordan River. And he said to the Israelites, "Someday, when your children ask you, 'Why are these stones so important?' tell them, 'The Jordan stopped flowing in front of the ark of the covenant of YAHWEH—the floodwaters were completely cut off.' These stones will serve as a memorial for Israel forever" (Joshua 4:6–7). Now that's a miracle! Not only did the water roll back, but God dried up the mud. The bottom of the river was dry. God's people didn't even get muddy. This was an impossibility! But impossibility is God's specialty.

He did this so that all the peoples of the earth might know that the hand of the Lord is powerful. And Joshua said, "These stones will serve as a memorial for Israel forever"—a powerful memorial to remind God's people that he has the power to keep every promise no matter how impossible it may seem.

The crossing over of the Israelites out of the wilderness into the promised land was a giant leap forward for them in every way. No longer were they to be mere nomads just getting by, but when they crossed the Jordan River, they were to take their place as a powerful nation on the world stage. This was the beginning of God's redemptive plan for them as a people of divine purpose. We already know the rest of the story. And we know that if Israel had not become a nation, then we would not have had a Messiah, our Lord Jesus, Yeshua. We would not have had a sin-conquering Savior. We would not have had the sacrifice that would bring us our salvation. So, we are thankful that Israel crossed over.

Twelve men were chosen to pick up stones from out of the middle of the river as they passed through and to bring the stones with them to the other side. These were to be stones of a good size, ones they had to carry on their shoulders. So, twelve men carried twelve stones from the river bottom, and they walked eight miles to Gilgal carrying them on their shoulders. When they got to Gilgal, Joshua set the stones up as a monument before God. He set then up as a memorial for the generations to come. Then when future generations asked, "What are these stones?" the people could retell this miraculous story. And they would be the evidence of the powerful God who can do anything and everything. This was one of the most awesome and glorious miracles in all the Word of God.

The number of the stones is significant, and the place where they set up the stones is significant as well. They carried out twelve stones upon their shoulders. Twelve is the number of divine government, and, as we noted earlier, the shoulder is a place of authority. God's house is going to be built out of living stones (1 Peter 2:5), which will establish his order on earth and in heaven. And the place where they set up the stones, Gilgal, can be translated as "a wheel" or "circle," which is also a picture of the government of God. His government and kingdom will be established through his house of faith, the people of God.

Did you know that the place where Joshua put those stones by the river is the same place where John the Baptizer baptized during the time Jesus was on the earth? In Matthew 3:9, John the Baptizer said that God could raise up sons from "these stones" to worship God. John's baptism was at the very place where the Israelites crossed over into the land (see John 1:28). Could it be that John the Baptizer baptized a generation of Joshua overcomers right there at the very place of the monument stones? I believe it was. And today Yahweh is still building a temple from out of his people. We are his living stones being perfectly fitted together as his temple, and we are all connected to the head cornerstone, the Anointed One, Jesus Christ himself (see Ephesians 2:20).

Let's Pray

Lord Jesus, I want all that you have for me today. I want to cross over into the fullness of your life in me. Take me in by your grace and show me the riches of your glory that you have deposited into my soul. You are my Rock, Fortress, and Defender. I come to rest my heart in your mercy and your love for me. Thank you for being all that I ever need! In your holy name. Amen.

16

JERICHO

We can demolish every deceptive fantasy that opposes God and break through every arrogant attitude that is raised up in defiance of the true knowledge of God. We capture, like prisoners of war, every thought and insist that it bow in obedience to the Anointed One.

2 CORINTHIANS 10:5

The very first stronghold the Israelites had to face in the promised land was Jericho. And we, too, have the same kind of stronghold to face when we go to claim our own inheritance. First, we must face the walled city and high places in our hearts and take them down. We find them in our thoughts.

Jericho is a picture of the stronghold of the mind because the mind is the very thing that keeps many Christians back. They choose to believe the lies that the enemy has fed them. Thoughts that say, *I'm not good enough. I'm like a grasshopper in the sight of giants. I have no way to stand up to them. I can't do it. I'm all alone in this. I don't have the resources.* These are all lies that can take over our thoughts. We often believe that it's all up to us. But it isn't up to us at all. The victory has already been won. God has already promised you, *Every place where you march, I've already given it to you* (see Joshua 1:3).

The Israelites went around the city of Jericho seven times just as the Lord had instructed, and they proved the word of the Lord to be true. It was their obedience to God that brought them their victory, for he was faithful to his word. He demolished the stronghold of Jericho right before everyone's eyes.

Our carnal minds are a picture of Jericho's walls. They represent the strongholds of insecurity, unbelief, doubt, fear, inability, and insufficiency. It's a picture of living in the land of not enough. It's always feeling like you have to strive to survive. You may feel you are surviving but not thriving. Existing but never able to dream. Holding on and failing to believe for more. God wants to bring all our Jericho walls down.

But there are two types of walls that the Lord does like: the walls of salvation (see Isaiah 60:18) and the wall of God's fiery presence all around us (see Zechariah 2:5). These two walls need to replace your Jericho walls. God wants you to allow him to erect these two walls around you. He desires to encamp around you with his wall of salvation and wall of the living fire of his presence and glory. These are the only two walls he wants you to live behind. The walls in our mind, in our emotions, and in our thinking have got to come down, or we'll never enter into where God is calling us. If not, those walls will keep us from all the blessing, intimacy, and inheritance the Lord has planned for us.

THE STRONGHOLD OF INTIMIDATION

This nearly impregnable walled city of Jericho can also be a picture of intimidation. It represents the fear that gets stirred up within us when principalities and powers try to stand in our way. It's the *no I can't* in our minds. It's the decision to give up when the warfare seems too strong even though the battle has already been won in Christ. It's when the devil and demonic powers say to us, *This far and no more.* And we give them a pass. We give in and give up. Intimidation is always the bait of Satan. He's so predictable. Once you go down that road with him, you're on the road of defeat. The Scriptures say that we're not ignorant of his schemes, so why do we let him get this far with us? We must stand up to him in faith and believe what God tells us is true.

The enemy especially likes to send his flaming arrows of lies at you when you're trying to enter the holy place to worship. And he loves to send stones of intimidation and accusation when you're trying to stand against that walled city and shout it down with faith—the faith declaration that God has spoken the truth and you will not bend to the enemy's intimidation tactics. But remember Romans 10:8: "God's living message is very close to you, as close as your own heart beating in your chest and as near as the tongue in your mouth." Like Joshua, you are destined to bring down your enemies with a shout of victory!

THE ENEMY'S SMOKE SCREEN

The walled city of Jericho also pictures the web of deceit and darkness, of discouragement and despair that the devil himself has put before you. The list of "disqualifiers" is endless. We have all dealt with this mental chatter that erodes our faith. It reeks of fear and unbelief. We've got to shake off the vision of limited destiny, inability, and insufficiency. God can shape your future when you give him your mind. When your mind is full of hope-filled expectation, the victory has already been won.

It's time to believe again, Joshua generation! It's time to hope. It's time to believe that there is no walled city that can stand before the One sent from God. It's time to recognize the lies of the enemy for what they are, a deceptive smoke screen attempting to hide the truth that we have already won. We must begin to believe that we are the Joshua generation. We must begin to process, digest, and believe the revelation that we're sent to possess our inheritance. Then we can boldly say that we are an apostolic, prophetic generation sent to rise up and take what God has already possessed and given us. And in spite of what anyone might do to discourage us, we're going to go for it. Then the mountains will move, the giants will die, and the walls will fall. That is the kind of bold faith that will bring down a walled city. And it will release the promises of God that are a part of your future.

LET'S PRAY

God of Power and Might, I come today to borrow your strength. I want the faith that you offer. I want a boldness that is linked to your heart and to your plan for my life. I want to live differently, love more deeply, and win my battles victoriously. I know that I need you each moment, so come and strengthen my inner being with your might. I want the resurrection power of Jesus to flow through me now. Amen.

17

A Divine Pause

All the Amorite kings west of the Jordan and all the Canaanite kings along the coast of the Mediterranean Sea became terrified of the Israelites. For when they heard how YAHWEH miraculously dried up the Jordan so that the Israelites could cross over, all their courage melted away.

JOSHUA 5:1

All the enemies of Israel heard the news, and they were put on notice. They had heard about the miracle of the Jordan moving aside for the people of God to cross. Now they were in a real panic, knowing that the same God who had parted the Red Sea had also made a way through the Jordan. This was proof that God was almighty and that he could do anything. Yes, nothing is impossible for God or for those who call upon him.

Joshua and his men had to be thinking, *We're ready! We have the men to conquer Jericho. Let's march right in without delay to take over.* I'm sure the greatest military strategists of our day would have told the Hebrews to go for it and to build on the momentum that they had going for them. However, there was just one problem. God hadn't told them to go in yet. You see, God is not in a hurry. His ways are often far different from the way we think things need to be done. Our reasoning is often very different from God's. His perspective of things is higher than ours. He is never worried about the enemy or the problems the enemy presents. And his plans and his timing may not always make sense to us, but they will always bring us to victory.

A Cutting Away

God's winning strategy was far different than anyone could have dreamed. And it definitely was not the conventional wisdom, but it was heaven's wisdom. And heaven's wisdom always leads to success. How would you fight and conquer all your enemies? I would bet that you wouldn't have done it the way God did it. He told the Israelites to take out a sharp knife and cut away their flesh. His plan started with circumcision! And all the men were to be circumcised before going out to battle. They were to take the knife, which represents the Word of God, and they were to circumcise the flesh, which is a picture of putting the knife to the flesh of our Adam-life.

> At that time, Yahweh commanded Joshua, "Make knives of flint and circumcise[10] the men of Israel again."[11] So Joshua made stone knives and circumcised all the men at a place they named Circumcision Hill.[12] (Joshua 5:2–3)

Now let me ask you, how much of a conquering, mighty, warrior champion would you be after just being circumcised? You would not be ready to go anywhere, much less into battle. I mean, think about how vulnerable they were! God intentionally made them weak and vulnerable. Now it would be several days of recovery time before they would be ready to go into Jericho. They had felt so triumphant when crossing the Jordan. From a human perspective, it would have been the time to race right in, but God commanded, and they were obedient.

Why would God ask this of them? One reason was to restore their covenant relationship. Israel was a covenant nation, and circumcision was the sign of that covenant. God established this covenant with Abraham when he called Abraham out of Ur of the Chaldeans. When he sealed the covenant with Abraham, God gave him the sign of the covenant, which was circumcision. It made Abraham's descendants a marked people. The mark of the covenant on their bodies showed that they belonged to the Lord and that they would be his continuously. Their bodies, souls, minds, and spirits were to be God's alone. As new-covenant believers, we have a similar sign or token, and it's called baptism. In circumcision and in baptism, we have a picture of putting off the Adam-life of the flesh.

Here they were, just a few miles from Jericho. They were ready, willing, and excited to go in and take possession of the land. But by God's instruction, they were temporarily disabled, from the little boys to the oldest men. Now, the oldest would have been Joshua and Caleb because everybody else from the original generation died in the wilderness. And so it is today that we, as the Joshua generation, are also coming out of exile and going into our inheritance. We are also going to go in wounded. We may be saying, *Oh God, I'm broken. I want to get fixed.*

But God says, *No, I'm not going to fix you. I'm going to remove your flesh completely out of the way.*

It's true. God's not after making your flesh look better; I can promise you that. Your Adam-life—your flesh life—is not going to get more mature. We are living sacrifices who have left our old lives behind and who go in as victorious conquerors shining the light and life of his glory through our conquered flesh.

God is raising up the Joshua generation to be a conquering, overcoming generation that rises above the dysfunction, the insecurity, the self-focus, and all of the other issues that result from a self-centered way of living. This generation is going to be a generation that believes and surrenders to the Word of God. The things of the flesh have been cut off, and they've been baptized into the co-crucifixion of our Savior, Jesus Christ. So don't be surprised if God wounds you before he uses you!

> Through our union with him we have experienced circumcision of heart. All of the guilt and power of sin has been cut away and is now extinct because of what Christ, the Anointed One, has accomplished for us. (Colossians 2:11)

LET'S PRAY

Father, I thank you for cutting away from my heart all that hinders you from expressing your life in me. Thank you for my union with Christ, the Anointed Substitute who lives his pure life in me. I yield to the life of Jesus. I choose to walk in the Spirit and not in the flesh. I will be one set free from the darkness and deceit of the Adam-life. Thank you for making this real in me today. Amen.

18

A Time to Remember

*While encamped at Gilgal, not far from Jericho, the Israelites
celebrated the Feast of Passover in the evening of the fourteenth day
of the month of Abib. The very next day, they ate for the first time
food grown in Canaan—roasted grain and flatbread made without
yeast. On that day, when they ate the produce of the land, the
manna stopped falling from heaven. The Israelites never ate manna
again, but that year they enjoyed the fruit of the land of Canaan.*

JOSHUA 5:10-12

The Passover meal itself was meant to be a reminder that the
Israelites were a redeemed people. Here they were, after the circumcision of the men, in their wounded condition, celebrating
the feast. Sounds like church life to me! Here we are also in our
wounded condition, trusting in the blood of the Lamb.

Forty years earlier, they celebrated the Passover on the night of their deliverance from Egypt. But they hadn't observed the Passover during the time of their sojourn in the wilderness. It had been an entire generation, forty years, since they had seen or observed the Passover Feast. Their ancestors had all died in the wilderness, and only those who were under forty were left to enter the land. So, before they entered the land, they needed to honor God by remembering the sacrifice of the lamb that brought them out of Egypt.

No matter what great thing we do—whether we topple a major stronghold, cast out demons, perform mighty miracles, or whatever other wonderful work we might perform—may we always give honor where honor is due. For without God, nothing and none of these things are possible. We must always recognize our Author and Finisher. The Lord wanted them to have the Passover as a remembrance of what he did to make them the chosen generation, a nation of warriors. He wanted them to remember the price he paid to bring them out of Egypt. The blood is our healing, freedom, deliverance, and victory.

A New Diet Plan

God instructed Joshua to do three things after the people crossed over and set up their memorial stones in Gilgal. First, deal with the flesh. Take the Word of God (flint knife) and cut off everything from the past. Second, they were to observe the Passover and devote themselves afresh to the God who brought them out of Egypt. And third, they were to go on a new diet plan. They were now going to eat the grain, the produce of the promised land. They had to eat the roasted grain.

You see, in Egypt, they ate leeks, garlic, and onions. In the wilderness, they had manna. But the day after they celebrated the Passover, the manna stopped. What are you going to do if your manna, your heavenly provision, seems to stop? What happens when the Father chooses to bring a change as to how he provides and sustains you? Before we can grasp the new, we must let go of the old. The "old" may be good and certainly served its purpose, but the old can become our enemy if we refuse to embrace the new day.

When seasons change in our lives, God forces us to feed on new truth, not the stale bread of yesterday. In the wilderness, God fed the Israelites each day with supernatural flakes, frost-like flakes of manna falling from the sky. Now they must work the ground, plant a crop, and harvest it. God was not going to feed them any longer; now they were going to feed themselves.

When we are spiritually immature, we have a diet that will make us strong, just like infants and toddlers will eat things that they will never eat once they become adults. Who wants to go back to eating baby food? But when you mature, God feeds you a different diet, the food of champions. Manna is a picture of the earthly life of Jesus. He is the Manna, the Bread that came down from heaven to satisfy our soul. But the grain of Canaan is a picture of the heavenly life of Jesus now on the throne of glory. The grain teaches us of death and resurrection. In Genesis 37, Joseph dreamed of God's people like wheat, grain springing up with resurrection life. We now must feed our souls not simply on the earthly life of Jesus but also on the resurrection life that we now share co-enthroned with him. Eat the grain, my friend, and forget about yesterday's moldy bread!

Are you ready for the change that God wants to bring into your life? It will require more of you than before. All the Israelites needed to do to get manna was to go out their tent doors and gather it up. It was there waiting for them each morning. But to labor in the dirt to sow and harvest means sweat. It means diligence. It means labor. Many believe that since Jesus has done it all and "It is finished," that we no longer have any responsibilities. How wrong that is! The more God uses you, the more willing you are to be spent, labor more than others, and pray when others play. The Joshua generation will be known as those who bring a new day of glory to the earth not because they simply waited for it but because they pulled the hoped-for future into today. They bent time. They took the key of David and went into the reality of a future world and pulled it into today's world. If God's kingdom is worth anything, then it's worth everything.

Let's Pray

Lord Jesus, I feast on you today. I thank you for the changes you have brought into my life over the last few years. You are making me into a new person, and I am grateful. Today, I ask for the grace to give you my all, my best, and everything I have. My love for you is greater than any other love. Take me, empower me, and use me for your glory. Amen.

19

DIVINE ENCOUNTER

When Joshua was near Jericho, he looked up and saw standing in front of him a man holding a drawn sword. Joshua approached him and said, "Are you on our side or on our enemies'?" "Neither," he replied. "I have not come to take sides but to take charge. I am the Commander of YAHWEH's armies." At once, Joshua threw himself facedown to the ground and worshiped, and he said to him, "I will do whatever you command, my Lord."

JOSHUA 5:13–14

What an amazing scene! Joshua was undoubtedly worried about how he would break the walls of Jericho, so he went out at dusk to survey the landscape. All at once, he saw a strange man standing in front of him. So Joshua stepped closer and boldly asked him, "Are you for us or for our enemies?" (v. 13 NIV). He didn't realize that this armed warrior was actually the Lord himself. Theologians call it a Christophany, a pre-incarnate, pre-virgin-birth appearance of the Lord Jesus. He came down as a mighty man of war. He is, in fact, the Commander in Chief of the armies of heaven. God came down to meet with his man, Joshua, and he appeared to Joshua in battle array with his sword in his hand, dressed as a conqueror.

Jacob had met him as the God who wrestles. Now Joshua meets him as the Commander in Chief. Wherever you are in your life, God will come to you as the one you need at the time. Whatever issue is going on in your life, whatever your career is, whatever your ministry track or field is, believe me, God is the head of that. So, for this mighty warrior named Joshua, this eighty-year-old giant-conquering warrior who went into the land while everybody else said it couldn't be done, God appeared as a mighty warrior, and not just any mighty warrior, but the Commander in Chief.

While all the other men of Israel shrank away in craven fear from the challenges of Canaan, Joshua and Caleb were the ones who said, "Do not be afraid of the people of the land, because we will devour them. Their protection is gone, but the LORD is with us" (Numbers 14:9 NIV). Joshua was telling the people, "We're not grasshoppers! Those giants are going to be our dinner." And like Joshua, we, too, we will feed from the victory of Christ in conquering the Canaanites. We will be made stronger through every spiritual battle we face, but we must not forget who ultimately has procured our victories: the Commander in Chief, the Commander of Angel Armies.

> The Commander of YAHWEH's armies said to Joshua, "Remove your sandals, for you are standing on holy ground!" And Joshua obeyed. (Joshua 5:15)

Joshua aligned himself with his leader and with the armies of heaven. The Lord adjusted Joshua with this very first command. *Let your feet touch the dirt from which you were made. Touch your humanity. Understand who you are and whom it is you're talking with. Take your shoes off and understand that I'm the one who will take this territory I've destined for you. Drink in my holiness and who I am. For I will handle Jericho. But first, Joshua, are you aligned with me? Will you want to do it your way, or will you be my surrendered servant? I have not come to take sides. I have come to take charge!*

God was about to give Joshua a bewildering assignment. He was going to instruct Joshua to march around the city of Jericho for seven days. What a crazy way to win a battle! What a confusing battle strategy! Think about it. God, in his infinite wisdom, knew that in the future, he would have to tell Joshua all kinds of things—difficult things, confusing things. So God was trying to get it straight, right here in the beginning. He was saying, *Let's fix this right here at the start. I am the Commander of Angel Armies. Will you be one of my soldiers? Can I lead you, or are you going to balk at my will for you? Are you going to cry and whine when I tell you to do hard things?* God wants a leader he can trust, a submitted and yielded leader.

Three Lessons from Joshua's Encounter

1. Jesus never comes to take sides; he comes to take over. He comes to lead us. The very one who came to Joshua and spoke the words, "I am the Commander of Yahweh's armies," also tells us, "When you live separated from me you are powerless" (John 15:5). It's the same principle, and it's the same lesson, whether it's Joshua facing Jericho or the Joshua generation of

this day ready to possess the promises. Joshua was an experienced soldier; however, experience helps us very little in the kingdom of God. What experience can do is give you a false sense that you know what God wants to do. Experience may tell you that you've been there and done that, and that makes you feel self-sufficient. The moment we think we stand, that's when we fall.

2. Rest in his victory. He has already won every battle you haven't even fought yet. Why struggle when God tells us to rest? We don't have to strive. Striving is the sure mark of struggling in the flesh. The resurrection life in you is effervescent. It's buoyant. It came out of heaven. It's not bound to this earth. The law of the spirit of life has set us free from the law of sin and death (see Romans 8:2). The law of sin and death is like the law of gravity that holds us to our problems, holds us to our old identity. It says, *I don't recognize that I have already been set free.* When the Spirit of life comes into you, the Spirit of resurrection life, the very Spirit that raised Jesus from the dead, you are set free from the law of sin and death.

3. God required humility from Joshua. He told him, "Take off your sandals," and Joshua humbly bowed down. Because of that divine encounter, Joshua forever afterward walked in the awareness of God's holiness. His walk was consecrated. This is a plan for victory! Start by bowing to the Commander of

YAHWEH's armies and humbly get onto his program. If you want to see your walled cities topple, maybe you need to get your shoes off, bow in reverence, absorb holiness, and then you will be able to do the necessary warfare to gain that ground.

The Commander in Chief stood with the sword drawn in his hand and said to Joshua, "I have given Jericho, its king and mighty warriors into your hands" (Joshua 6:2). I "have given" Jericho into your hand. All that Joshua needed to do was simply to march forward, obeying the word of the Lord. Those of the Joshua generation are the ones who know the promises of God, believe the promises of God, and step out into the promises of God.

LET'S PRAY

Lord Jesus, I bow low before you. You will not take my side in my battles; rather, you will take charge. You have not come to "help me" but to deliver me from myself and my pride. I want you to be glorified in my life today. There is no enemy you cannot conquer and no battle that you cannot win. I yield my heart to you. I lower my shield and my sword to you alone. Mighty Warrior, come and be my victory today. Amen.

20

VICTORY AT JERICHO

Now the gates of Jericho were bolted and barred because of the Israelites; no one could get in or out. YAHWEH commanded Joshua, "See, I have given Jericho, its king and mighty warriors into your hands. March around the city with all your men of war once a day for six days. Have seven priests carry shofars in front of the ark. On the seventh day, march around the city seven times, with the priest blowing the shofars."

JOSHUA 6:1–4

It is time to go up and straight in. If you're trying to win, you've already lost. God doesn't want you to try to win. God wants you to stand in the victory that he has provided for you. God said to Joshua, "I have given you Jericho." The victory was guaranteed. Their shout was a shout of faith. They had already seen the city being conquered and given to them.

In the same way, Jesus Christ has already defeated every spiritual enemy for us. When Jesus was compelled to retreat into the wilderness, he fought the enemy of his soul for you and me (see Matthew 4). Christ Jesus won the battle for us on the cross. And he won the battle in his earthly ministry and cast out demons, healed sickness, and conquered all. Colossians 2:13–14 says that he has resurrected us out of the "realm of death," never to return. That's how powerful your Lord Jesus Christ is.

You fight not for victory but from a place of victory. Ephesians 6:13 says that when you are confronted by the slanderer and are wearing the armor of God, you "will rise victorious." Your victory has been secured by the cross and the resurrection. You stand complete through the victorious, triumphant ministry of our Lord Jesus Christ. You don't have a battle to win, only a victory to claim and implement by faith. Faith *is* the victory.

GOD'S INSTRUCTION

The very instruction of the Lord carries power. Joshua didn't take the city by a clever military tactic. He didn't build any catapults or battering rams. He didn't hire another army to help him because the Israelites' numbers were small. No, Joshua didn't use the clever tactics of men because the strategy was the Lord's, and Joshua believed him. British missionary James Hudson Taylor said that there are three ways to serve the Lord. Number one, make the best plans you can and hope they succeed. Number two, make your own plans and then ask God to bless them. Number three, ask God for his plans, do whatever he tells you to do, and then expect the blessings to overflow.[13]

God's plan for conquering Jericho was kind of bizarre and unexpected. But it was the plan of God, and that was enough. God's instruction was simply to march around the city. It looked foolish, but it worked because inherent within the instruction of God was the power of God to accomplish his will. Luke 1:37 promises, "Not one promise from God is empty of power. Nothing is impossible with God!" The plans of God may look strange, but they work. And God's method is for us to partner with him. He could do it alone, but he limits himself to partnership. It doesn't compute in our minds, but that's the way God has chosen. God wants you to sacrifice, obey, and follow the instructions of the Lord. So again, the victory roadmap we see in Joshua is clear—it's the fear of the Lord on his enemy, the promise of God in our hearts, and the instruction of the Lord in our feet as we walk it all out by faith and watch as his power comes to back him up.

TRUMPETS OF JUBILEE

> When you hear the blare of the shofars, have all the people shout with a mighty shout of joy! Then the walls of the city will collapse before your eyes, and your whole army must charge straight in! (Joshua 6:5)

Trumpets of rejoicing! The trumpet blast simply proclaimed that God had already given the city to the Israelites. It wasn't the power of the shofar or the shout or the marching of the people that caused such a great vibration that the city walls fell down. No, it was God's miracle power at work combined with the obedience of the people to his words.

The bizarre thing was that the walls fell forward toward the Israelites. They fell out because the blast came down from heaven. It wasn't the ground shaking or a sonic boom. It was the power of the authority of God and his people together. It was all accomplished through partnering; it was the march of obedience, the trumpet of jubilee, and the shout of faith working in partnership with the power of the Word. God's power can bring down any stronghold. Take the ram's horn of jubilee—the sound of victory—and blow! Blow it big and loud! Then, when you're finished, shout. Shout your victory. Release the shout of triumphant faith because God has given you the victory. And watch his power demolish that thing that has held you. Faith releases his power and the victory.

The victory shout of praise conquered the enemy. It destroyed the stronghold of darkness that held the walls of Jericho. Jericho was perhaps the citadel, the headquarters of central Palestine where the Canaanites were, but it was one of *many*. There were other cities, yet it was through the destruction of Jericho that the sound went through the entire land in the spirit realm. The collapse of Jericho's walls reverberated throughout the land, and from that moment on, everything else became a mop up operation. The victory had already been given to the Israelites by God. So, never doubt the power of your praise.

LET'S PRAY

Father God, give me the grace to walk the pathway of the Joshua generation. I acknowledge that I am buried and crucified with Jesus. My life is not my own. I pray, Lord, that you would help me to remember my Redeemer and Rescuer, who sacrificed himself for me so that I could begin to feed on the heavenly grain, the new diet of the land, digesting the deeper truths of the cross, the revelation that will set me free and make me Christlike. Oh Commander of YAHWEH's armies, I acknowledge that you're in charge and you're the one who dispenses victory. Knock down my walls and all of my strongholds. Take charge. I bow in loving reverence before you. Yes! I am willing to take orders. I submit myself to you. Amen.

21

FAITH IS THE VICTORY

Joshua son of Nun summoned the priests and instructed them:
"Take up the ark of the covenant, and have seven priests carry
seven shofars in front of the ark of YAHWEH."
And to the people he said, "Forward! March around the city and
set an advance guard of armed men to march ahead of the ark of
YAHWEH."
At Joshua's order, the seven priests carrying seven shofars advanced
before YAHWEH. The ark of the covenant of YAHWEH followed
them as they made long blasts on their shofars. The advance guard
marched in front of the priests who were blowing the shofars, the
rear guard marched behind the ark, and the shofars blared the
whole time!

JOSHUA 6:6–9

Think back. Did the ark follow the people into the promised land? No. The Israelites followed the ark. The ark went into the Jordan first, and the waters were pushed back to the city of Adam, and God's people came into their promised inheritance. Just about the time you think you have God's ways figured out, he seems to change things. And this is how we begin to learn to walk by faith and obedience. It's a partnership, not a program to follow. This time Joshua ordered the people to advance and march around the city with the armed guard proceeding the ark of the Lord. They were leading and taking God into their battle. And so it is in our daily lives that we can take God into the midst of our hardest difficulties, our issues, and seeming impossibilities.

SACRED SILENCE

> Now Joshua had commanded the rest of the people, "Do not shout! Remain silent! Don't make a sound until the moment I command you to shout. Then lift up a shout with all your might!" So the ark of YAHWEH circled the city once, then they all came back to the camp in Gilgal and spent the night. (vv. 10–11)

So, the ark of the Lord was silently carried around the city. After circling Jericho once, the people returned to the camp and spent the night there. This went on for a week. It was a miracle that the people kept their mouths shut, and they only shouted when God told them to. Try to imagine a million people hushed for God. God's spirit is about to fall on the Joshua generation, and we're not going to let a sound out of our mouths until God gives it to us. And when he does, our sound will pierce the heavens and conquer cities with the gospel.

> On the second day, they circled the city once and again returned to the camp. They repeated this pattern for six days. (v. 14)

Then, on the seventh day, things changed:

> On the seventh day, everyone rose at daybreak, and they marched around the city in the same manner seven times. After their seventh time around, when the priests were about to blow the shofars, Joshua commanded the people: "Shout a shout of joy! YAHWEH has given you the city! Jericho and everything in it are to be a devoted offering to YAHWEH." (vv. 15–17)

Now imagine a massive army with the ark, trumpets, the armed men in the front, and the rear guard behind, marching around with the people. The seventh time around, when the priests sounded the trumpet blast, Joshua commanded the people, "Shout a shout of joy! YAHWEH has given you the city!"

Here's the question: What would you do for victory and breakthrough? What would you do to see your walled city crumble? What would you be willing to do in order to see strongholds that keep you from the truth come crashing down? Would you shout? Would you pray? You must do whatever God tells you to do. It requires an act of obedient faith. We must find out God's plan and execute it. When we accept God's plan, we're inviting God's presence, and when God's presence comes, he brings victory with him. Breakthrough is found in his presence. As we merge with God and our wills become one, strongholds crumble and the walled cities fall.

> The people were ready to shout with a great shout when they heard the shofars. As soon as they heard

the blast of the shofars, they raised a massive shout
of jubilee like a thunderclap, and all at once the
thick walls of Jericho collapsed! Everyone rushed
straight ahead and captured the city. (v. 20)

The Israelites overcame the enemy by faith. By faith, the walls
of Jericho fell down when the people followed God's command
and did exactly as he said. And the other part of what God told
them to do was this:

Jericho and everything in it are to be a devoted
offering to YAHWEH. But spare Rahab the prostitute and everyone in her house because she hid
our spies. You must not take for yourselves anything that is dedicated to YAHWEH or you will
bring trouble and destruction to the entire Israelite
camp! Everything made of silver, gold, bronze,
and iron is sacred and devoted to YAHWEH; place
all of it in YAHWEH's treasury!...

They utterly destroyed all that was in Jericho,
men and women, young and old, livestock and
donkeys—everything was destroyed with the
sword. (vv. 17–19, 21)

When we obey God's command, we win. Yet God is the one
who procures the victory, so all the glory belongs to him, and we
need to offer it up to bring honor where honor is due. All the
treasure must go into God's treasury. So, the Israelites devoted
the city to the Lord and destroyed with the sword every living
thing in it: men and women, young and old, cattle, sheep, and
donkeys. It was all devoted to the Lord. Here is the lesson for us:
obey God's commands and give him the glory when the victory

comes. This is a picture of the truth that every barrier, every hindrance that is standing on your inheritance has to be destroyed. No mercy, no toleration, no quarter to the enemy. We don't compromise. We don't spare what we want to spare. We don't say, *I'll get rid of everything…except this, Lord. I'll let every relationship in my life be devoted to you except this one because it is so meaningful to me.* No, it doesn't work like that. It's all or nothing. God will have no other idol in your heart. He will have no competitor. Even our relationships must be in line with God's purposes for our lives. Total consecration is the picture here. You are called to be his burning one! You must throw into the fire everything that distracts you from him.

LET'S PRAY

God of Glory, every victory in my life is because of you. It is not by my might or by my power but by your Spirit. I owe everything to you and devote everything I am to you today. I hold nothing back, nothing. I live for you and for you alone. Take my heart and make it your holy sanctuary. Live through me. Not I, but Christ. Amen.

22

God's Victory Weapons

Faith pulled down Jericho's walls.

Hebrews 11:30

The victory of Jericho was a great miracle. The walls came tumbling down not because they were battered down but because God's people were obedient. Similarly, the strongholds in your life are not going to come down because you are wise or clever, not because your natural weapons are powerful, but the strongholds are going to come down because Christ is in you and, in him, nothing is impossible. There is no barrier that can keep him back except your own heart. But when you walk in agreement with him, nothing is impossible.

Who knocked the walls down? God did! The walls of Jericho came down because God was among his people. But God's people had to cooperate for it to happen. They marched around the city for six days, about a two-mile walk. And on the seventh day, they walked around the city seven times at the instruction of the Lord. God's weapons were not the normal, conventional military might. The weapons that the Hebrews used to destroy the mighty walled city of Jericho were the ark carried on the priests' shoulders, the blowing of the trumpets, the shout of faith, and the unity of God's people. This may seem strange to the natural mind, yet they were God's powerful weapons at the time. Let's look at these divine weapons.

THE ARK ON OUR SHOULDERS

The ark carried on the shoulders of the priests was a symbol of an important truth. The ark represented the priests carrying God into the battle. Are you taking God into the battles of your thought life and your heart? It isn't just a formula that you follow. And it isn't just a clever strategy or a ritual of prayer. It's actually an intimate connection with God. We need God's presence in order to have success.

THE SHOUT OF FAITH

The shout was a symbol of their faith. Shouting before you see the victory is so significant. Before the victory is when most people get depressed. That's usually when things are at their worst and everything is falling apart. It's that time when there seems to be no hope, no answer in the natural realm, and there's no way out. When the situation is absolutely at its worst, God says, *Shout! Shout the shout of faith. Shake the stronghold over your life with your roar of faith and watch what I will do.* Release the sound of heaven into the earth, and you will see demonic obstacles fall.

THE UNITY OF GOD'S PEOPLE

Unity is the blessing releaser. It is one of the most overlooked weapons from Joshua 6. God's people were together. Yes, the greatest miracle in the book of Joshua is not that the sun stood still. The greatest miracle is that a million people walked around the city with their mouths shut for an entire day! They walked in unity, and they didn't fuss or grumble. They marched in obedience around the city. And God delighted in what he saw: a people of faith and courage, trusting God and knit together in love and unity.

WALKING IN GOD'S SEVENTH DAY

There was no visible result of their literal steps of obedience until *the seventh day.* Sometimes you've got to step out and obey God even when there are no physical signs of victory. You won't always see the victory at first. For example, the first time you read your Bible, the first week you begin to tithe to your church, or the first time you cut loose with the shout of faith may not necessarily show any promising results. It takes obedience. But with continued, consistent obedience, you will begin to see things move. In this case, it was not the first day, the second day, the fourth day, or even the fifth day—it was the seventh day when the miracle came. Seven represents completeness. We need to walk in God's seventh day, the day he rested in his completed, perfect work.

OBEDIENCE

When we walk in obedience, we're resting in faith and walking in unity with God's people until it's time to shout. When we obey what God has said, we can be sure our victory is coming. The seventh day is coming! The Israelites triumphed, and so it will come for you. God had already given the city into the hands of Joshua. It was his to take. So, on the seventh day, with seven priests, with seven trumpets, carrying the ark of glory, and the seventh time around the city, they shouted the shout of faith and realized their victory.

Hear this today: get ready to be surprised at how God wins your victory and how God breaks through for you. He's going to touch your life and bring forth his glory. And it's not going to be the same way as before. It's going to be different. For he is famous for using methods and people who demonstrate that it is God, and God alone, who wins their battles.

God chooses us, the foolish ones, and he often uses methods that seem foolish to others to bring forth his glory on the earth. I mean, look at the people he uses. He even chose each one of us. This so clearly shows that he is not looking for our strength, wisdom, or ability. He just wants our obedient love. God is so amazing! If you're weak, then you're a prime candidate for victory. You're the very one God's been looking for. For the problem has never been that you're too weak. It's that you're too strong for God to use. God delights in human weakness. He loves to use frail, broken people because his glory then can come through, and they won't steal it for themselves. For it's then that we can say to every-body, "God is the one who won the victory!"

It wasn't the catapult or crossbow that won the victory for the Israelites. It wasn't the powerful weapons of this world. No, it was the shout of faith. Faith in an all-good, all-powerful, almighty God. God's people shouted up, and God's blast came down from heaven. The walls of Jericho fell out, and the people went over the wall and into the city and took it. You see, it was this microburst of glory that flattened down the city...except one household, the household of Rahab.

So, they rescued only one family from destruction in the entire city of Jericho, the family of the prostitute Rahab. To us, saving a prostitute and her family might seem strange. But God thinks differently. He chooses the weak, the helpless, the broken, the people who have nothing and who turn to him. He chooses those who cannot boast about themselves, the "Rahabs" that the world disqualifies. It's when we try to be somebody that God leaves. And it's when we think our cleverness will give us the victory we so desire that we fail.

LET'S PRAY

Father, I come in my weakness, acknowledging that I have no strength but in you. My glorious Lord, you are the strength of my life. As I face each day, you promise that I will have your strength to overcome and walk in victory. I lean my heart into yours. I want my life to testify today of your greatness. Live your life of victory and power through me. Amen.

23

Rahab, a Woman of Faith

Joshua spared Rahab the prostitute, her father's family, and all that belonged to her. She lives among the Israelites to this day because she hid the two men Joshua sent to spy out Jericho.

Joshua 6:25

Faith provided a way of escape for Rahab the prostitute, avoiding the destruction of the unbelievers, because she received the Hebrew spies in peace.

Hebrews 11:31

Rahab was a woman of faith listed in the Hall of Faith in Hebrews 11. She found favor with a holy God because of her faith. Yes, she was a prostitute, yet she is included right along with the "saints" like Enoch, Noah, Abraham, Moses—all mentioned in Hebrews 11. She had faith, incredible, saving, dynamic, bold faith. But she had an entirely different journey than the others listed.

Rahab was a prostitute, so what do you do with a story like hers? God's ways are higher than ours. Bible scholars have gone around and around over Rahab. There are all kinds of commentaries on her, and over 50 percent of them say that Rahab was not really a harlot and that the word *harlot* actually means "innkeeper." They say she owned a bed-and-breakfast, and she was surely a respectable businesswoman. That's really cool until you turn to the book of James, where she is clearly named as a "prostitute."

> The same is true of the prostitute named Rahab who was found righteous in God's eyes by her works, for she received the spies into her home and helped them escape from the city by another route. (James [Jacob] 2:25)

God led the two spies right to her house. Can you imagine being one of those spies? You are on a strategic, world-changing mission from God, and he sovereignly and surprisingly sends you to this woman for help. They end up at the doorstep of a prostitute's house. Of all the people in the city. It probably didn't do a lot for their reputation, but it did for hers!

That day changed the course of her life forever. Eventually she married a Hebrew man by the name of Salmon, and they had a baby boy named Boaz. And Boaz married Ruth, and they had a boy named Obed, who got married and had a son called Jesse. And Jesse had a son named David. This made Rahab the great-great-grandmother of King David. She is listed in Matthew 1, included in the divine genealogy of our Lord Jesus Christ. But the most important thing about Rahab is also the most important thing about you, and that's your faith. It isn't an anointing or talent. It's your faith in action that makes you a part of the Joshua generation.

THE FAITH OF RAHAB

So, what kind of faith did Rahab have? She had a *courageous* faith. If you're going to have faith, why not make it courageous? Rahab exhibited an "all-or-nothing" kind of faith. Before the spies even arrived in Jericho, Rahab had turned from idols to serve the living and true God. She was a person whom everybody had written off and nobody in a million years would have included in the genealogy of the Messiah, but God is not like us. God has chosen the weak things of the world to put to shame the things that are mighty. God chooses "Rahabs."

Do you realize how famous God is when he uses you in your weakness? It's God, not your cleverness, not your spiritual gift, or your beauty that you get to display on the platform. It's a weak, frail, broken person who can hardly live right one week to the next. Jesus was a friend of publicans and sinners. It's amazing, isn't it? In the upside-down/right-side-up world of God, things are truly set right. Step into God's reality, and suddenly everything looks different. *It's totally different...but perfect.* The impossible becomes possible. And the reward of having him outweighs outrageous risk. That's what Rahab discovered. So she willingly risked her own life when she welcomed the spies. Rahab's faith was courageous!

CONQUERING FAITH

Indeed, Rahab was a woman of great, fear-conquering faith. She wasn't a theologian, but look at her doctrine: "YAHWEH, your

God, is the true God who rules in heaven above and on earth below" (Joshua 2:11). These weren't the words of a Bible scholar but a pagan, female prostitute. She never heard any sermons. Had never been taught about her calling or destiny. She only knew one thing: the God of the Israelites was the true God. Rahab was living in this citadel of darkness surrounded by her sin and by the pagan lifestyle of moon worshiping Jerichoites. While sitting in spiritual darkness, she begins to hear the news of what God had done through Moses in bringing the Israelites out of Egypt and the parting of the Red Sea forty years earlier. That news was still reverberating in the city of Jericho, and it birthed faith in her heart because "faith comes by hearing, and hearing by the word of God" (Romans 10:17 NKJV). She heard and she believed. Rahab was one in a million. She believed the report of the Lord. Faith was birthed in her heart, and it changed her destiny forever.

Compassionate Faith

Rahab had a compassionate faith. First of all, she showed her compassionate faith when she took in the Hebrew spies. If the word had gotten out that the two spies whom Joshua had sent were in her house, it would have meant death for her. And if the king of Jericho had caught them in her house, her life would have been over, but still she had compassion. She saw the danger, but she brought them into her house anyway.

And her compassion also shows when she asks that her family be saved. She has no husband or children that we know of; therefore, the family she mentions here is not her husband and kids. She is referring to her father and her mother, her brothers and her sisters. This meant that her family would hereafter become included among the Hebrews. She wanted that for her family. By faith she had hope for a new beginning, a new life.

When Rahab eventually came out of Jericho, the walls had fallen. They fell all around. But there was one sliver of a wall left, the one sliver of the wall where Rahab's house was located. Talk about a miracle! It wasn't just a miracle that the walls of Jericho fell over. The miracle was that the walls of Jericho fell over *except* where there was a scarlet rope hanging from one window. Some of the miracle-denying scholars actually attribute Jericho's fall to an earthquake. But what kind of earthquake does that? One commentary claims that all of the marching feet for seven days going around Jericho began to crack the foundation, and that's why the walls shook. Then the people shouted, and the reverberation of the noise and the volume and the stomping of the feet made the walls fall down.

There were actually two walls, an outer and an inner wall. The first wall was thirty feet high and six feet wide. The second wall was thirty feet high and twelve feet wide. There are reports that the city wall was so thick that chariots could be driven along the top of it; historians have written about it. The wall was that substantial. Twelve feet thick! This was a fortress. Yet, the finger of God brought it down like it was nothing while simultaneously preserving one segment where Rahab lived with her family. Rahab is an example of how God can convert the most degraded people and make them part of his eternal family. Aren't you glad that has happened to you?

LET'S PRAY

Father, you have saved my soul and given me eternal life. I don't deserve your grace, but I rejoice in all that you have given me. I ask that you help me to be grateful and to see you in the big and little things that come into my life. Give me eyes that focus on your goodness. Amen.

24

THE PITFALL OF PRIDE

"You must not take for yourselves anything that is dedicated to
YAHWEH *or you will bring trouble and destruction to the entire*
Israelite camp!"

JOSHUA 6:18

We are always the most vulnerable right after a victory because it's then that we're most tempted to become self-reliant. We can begin to think that we just escaped something that was horrible, and so now we've broken free into a new place. Beware! Those are the moments when we're the most susceptible to spiritual attack. Now that we've tasted victory, we can't afford to go back and think that we can rest on our own accomplishments.

What did God command the Hebrews to do when they went into Jericho after the walls came down? They were to go into the city and burn it entirely, but they were not to take anything of value. The city and its valuables were to be fully devoted as a sacrifice to God. This was a heavy instruction! If one person were to take even one thing for himself from the city of Jericho, then the entire camp of Israel would be liable to destruction. If one sinned, God would judge the whole camp. You see, it was not merely the spoils of battle that God required; it was the devotion of everyone and everything to God.

When God brings victory in our life, it is a devoted thing, meaning that it is for God alone and to his glory alone. It's *through* God and it's *to* God that all things must be. Jericho was to be given over to God in sacred devotion to him. Everything in the city—animals, people, everything—was to be totally surrendered to God alone.

Failure in the Land of Promise

> The Israelites violated the commandment regarding the wealth of Jericho that was to be set apart for the Lord. Achan son of Carmi, grandson of Zimri, of the clan of Zerah, from the tribe of Judah, stole some of the devoted things for himself. This ignited Yahweh's anger against Israel. (Joshua 7:1)

How would you like to bring disgrace not only on your own name but also on your father's name, your grandfather's, and your great-grandfather's name—all disgraced because of *your* sin and disobedience. Achan's whole lineage was marked by his sin. He took some of the devoted things, and because of this, the Lord's anger burned against all of Israel, causing them to experience an unnecessary defeat even while they were in the land of victory. In this short but tragic story, there are three key components we're going to take a look at: the disobedient soldier (Achan), a defeated army, and the result of a discouraged leader (Joshua). Let's see what we can learn from Achan's disobedience.

A Disobedient Soldier

The name Achan means "trouble." Achan, Achor, or Achar are all derivatives of the same word or the same name, like Jim, James, and Jimmy. It's all the same in the Hebrew language. Achan is and will be forever known as the man in the Bible who troubled Israel. Because of his disobedience, he single-handedly defeated the entire nation. One man sinned and took what was not his, brought sin into the entire camp, and provoked God's anger against the whole nation.

Because of the disobedience of Achan, Israel was defeated at Ai. God's people had seen nothing but victory up until Ai. They had seen the waters of the Jordan rolled back, and they had seen the walls of Jericho fall down miraculously, and so they had no reason to expect anything other than victory. Up until this time they had not experienced defeat. Unfortunately, they took God's favor and miracles lightly, and they stepped into pride and presumption.

The Hebrew word *Ai* means "a heap of ruins." It's a picture of the world in its compromise and sin—*a heap of ruins*! Joshua moved ahead into the city after his spies returned to him with a report that Ai was nothing compared to Jericho. After all, Jericho was the city that was the greatest stronghold in the land. It was the capital of Canaan, an important city. So, they reasoned that Ai was so small and the inhabitants so few that they wouldn't worry about mustering their entire army but send only a portion, two or three thousand of their best troops, to conquer the city.

> They reported to [Joshua], "There is no need to
> trouble the whole army to conquer Ai. The people
> are so few that two or three thousand men could
> attack it and take the city." (v. 3)

Notice they said nothing about taking the ark, and there is no mention of prayer. There's no mention of seeking God or of humbling their hearts. Watch out when you've just had a victory! Be careful that you don't begin to believe that it was something you did in your own strength. It's when we think we stand that we are the most susceptible to a fall. In the afterglow of victory, pride often enters our heart. That's what happened in Israel. A subtle pride began to rise up. They may have thought, *We saw the walled city fall down without even losing a single person. And we conquered the entire city without a weapon. We didn't use a sword, a spear, or an arrow.* Even though they understood it was by the power of God, their pride began to creep in. So, they went up to Ai. Only three thousand men went, and the people of Ai beat them badly, killing thirty-six Israelites. The Hebrew says "thirty and six." Thirty is the number of maturity, and six is the number of man. This was the fullness of man's wisdom, man's cleverness, man's ideas and strategies, but without God.

> So Joshua sent three thousand troops to attack the
> city, but they were routed by the men of Ai. The
> men of Ai chased them from the city gates, down
> the hill as far as the quarries, cutting them down
> as they fled. They killed thirty-six of Joshua's men,
> and when Israel heard of their defeat, their hearts
> melted away with fear! (vv. 4–5)

What was their mistake? They thought that they could conquer Ai with just a few people and without the ark of God's glory leading them in victory. Let me ask you: What is *your* boast? Your greatest curse is often your greatest strength. Self-confidence that is not rooted in the wisdom or power of God wants to make us think that we can handle everything all on our own. Pride will always lead us to defeat.

A Discouraged Leader

So not only was there a disobedient soldier and a defeated army, but now Joshua was also discouraged. This was his first defeat, and he prostrated himself in real despair before the ark of God. The Bible says that he fell down before the ark, weeping and crying.

> Joshua and the elders of Israel tore their clothes and threw dust over their heads to show their sorrow. They threw themselves facedown to the ground in front of the ark of Yahweh until the evening sacrifice. (v. 6)

If Joshua had fallen down before the ark like he fell down before the Commander of Angel Armies before they marched around Jericho and had gotten his directed orders from God first, there would have been an entirely different outcome. But you and I often do the same thing as well. We get a victory in our life, begin to take ground spiritually in one area or another, and before long, a subtle over-confidence comes in. We seek the presence of the Lord less and less as we begin to move in our own wisdom. Why? Because we think we're experienced and we've been in the church for a long time. Look out! The Holy Spirit flows through those who yield, not those who are know-it-alls and full of themselves. If we're filled with our own self-confidence, how can God give us anything? It's only as we yield to him that we walk in continuous victory.

LET'S PRAY

Almighty God, I humble myself before you. I know that I am weak, powerless, and unable to win the battle that is in front of me today. It is not by my might nor by my power but by your Spirit that I overcome. Help me. Remind me throughout my day that it is only by your Spirit, your life in me, that I win the victory. Amen.

25

SIN IN THE CAMP

Joshua cried out, "O Lord YAHWEH, why did you lead these people across the Jordan? To be defeated? To be killed by the Amorites? If only we had been content to stay on the other side of the Jordan!
O Lord, what can I say now that Israel has retreated from its enemies? When the Canaanites and everyone else in the land hear about our defeat, they will gang up on us and wipe us off the face of the earth. And what then will you do about your great name?"

JOSHUA 7:7–9

Does that sound familiar? Have you ever wondered, *God, why did you do this to me? Why did you mess up my life? Why did you let this happen? Why did I have to go through this?* If self-pity is a problem in your life, receive this counsel: get up in the name of the Lord! As Jesus said, "Pick up your mat and walk" (John 5:8 NIV). Now is the time to take it up and walk into the light of God.

> YAHWEH spoke to Joshua: "Stand up! Why are you
> groveling before me? Israel has sinned! They have
> broken the covenant which I had commanded
> them to keep. They have taken forbidden plunder.
> They have stolen from me, taken what is mine, hid-
> den it among their belongings, and lied about it.
> (Joshua 7:10–12)

Sin in the camp devastated the Israelites' ability to stand as
one obedient body. Instead, compromise had perforated the can-
opy of grace over their camp and had let in darkness, defeat, and
discouragement so that the enemies of God defeated them. And
it was all because of hidden compromise. They turned back on
the day of battle, and they fled. God was saying, "I'm not going to
cover you in my mercy and grace until you deal with the sin. It's
keeping my victory from being manifest. And unless you do what
I've told you to do, there will be only defeat."

> Get up and purify the people in preparation for
> tomorrow. Tell them, "This is what YAHWEH, the
> God of Israel says: 'O Israel, you have in your midst
> what must be devoted entirely to me! You cannot
> stand against your enemies until you remove the
> devoted things from among your midst!'" (v. 13)

God's wisdom and instruction is this: you will never defeat
your enemies until you relinquish those things that should be
devoted to him. It's really simple. God expects obedience. Yes,
we're covered with grace. Yes, mercy drips from the skies. Yes, new
mercies are indeed fresh and real and unveiled every morning. But
sometimes the trouble that comes into our lives is because we've
brought it on ourselves. Hidden compromise—those issues that

we've refused to address and things we knew we were supposed to do but didn't bother to do—will bring defeat into our lives.

Israel had to deal with sin. They had to go back to the camp and find out who had compromised. The tribes of Israel would never be able to claim their inheritance as long as one man held on to forbidden treasure. The people of God weren't going to be able to enter the promised land as long as they clung to what was forbidden. Have we given everything to him or not? How can we be so stupid? And how can we expect the ark of glory to lead us into triumph and a victory in our life when we're lying? The Joshua generation cannot move forward in victory until they remove the sin from the camp. They were stopped in their tracks at the "heap of ruins" because they had failed to take God into the battle. They took their own experience. They relied on their clever strategy and not on the presence of God.

Uncovering the Problem

So Joshua sent the word throughout the camp and told them to assemble everybody to have a moment of reckoning. The problem was hidden somewhere in their camp in plain sight, and it was Joshua's duty to discover it. Joshua called forward every tribe, and God spoke to Joshua as each tribal leader passed by Joshua. God would show Joshua which tribe was guilty of hiding sin in the camp.

The process of elimination began. When finally the family of Judah passed before Joshua, the Lord said, "This is the tribe." Then, all the families of the tribe of Judah passed before the Lord, and the Lord spoke and said, "It's the clan of Zerah." Then Joshua had all the families of Zerah present themselves before the Lord, and God spoke to Joshua and said, "It is the family of Zabdi." And Joshua told all the men in the family of Zabdi to present themselves before the Lord. There were perhaps seven, eight, ten men in that family. Can you imagine how they must have felt? Here they are standing before the Lord and before Joshua, and the Lord indicates to Joshua that it was Achan, the man of trouble, son of Carmi. Nobody can hide from God. It doesn't matter if you are a pastor, priest, or anyone else. Not one of us is exempt from the gaze of God. Before the eyes of "him with whom we have to do" (Hebrews 4:13 KJV), we will all pass, and God himself will inspect our hearts.

God's methodical approach singled out first the tribe, then the clan, then the family, then the household, and finally the culprit himself, Achan. He was the offender, and everybody stood looking at him now, wondering, *What did this guy do to bring defeat at Ai?*

> Then Joshua said to Achan, "My son, give glory to Yahweh, the God of Israel, and confess. Tell me the truth and do not hide anything from him. What have you done?"
>
> "It's true," Achan said. "I've sinned against Yahweh, the God of Israel. This is what I did." (Joshua 7:19–20)

Achan said, "It's true." You see, confessing his sin was not so that God could figure it out as if God were merely going on a hunch. No, the Lord knew that it was Achan. The confession of the sin was important for two reasons: so that Achan would deal with his sin and so that the people of God would deal with the sin issue in their midst. God is always glorified when we confess known sin.

ACHAN'S TENT

> I saw among the plunder an exquisite robe from
> Babylon, two hundred pieces of silver, and a fifty-
> shekel bar of gold. I wanted them badly, so I took
> them and buried them in my tent with the silver
> underneath. (v. 21)

Joshua then discovered the evidence. He went to the tent of Achan, and he found three things: a Babylonian garment, silver, and gold. It must have been very attractive and valuable. Part of the allure was that it was a *mantle,* a robe. Mantles represent callings and appointments of God. *Achan lusted for a mantle.* He was trying to take the mantle that was not his. You see, God is the one who distributes mantles. He's the one who releases garments of righteousness, garments of prophetic revelation, and mantles of callings. This is a symbolic warning to us not to lust or be jealous for someone else's gift or somebody else's prophetic revelation. To do so is to go after something that is not ours. Our callings are given to us by God. He makes our callings and elections sure.

And Achan stole silver, two hundred shekels of silver and a wedge of gold. The Hebrew is literally "a tongue of gold." He took a fifty-shekel hunk of gold. I wonder how he could carry all this. Think about the time, the effort, and all the deceit involved with this escapade. He probably had to transport each item to his tent one at a time. All this effort now counted to his demise. God saw it all. This was no ordinary shoplift. Achan took what God said was to be devoted to YAHWEH. And lest any of us think this is something that we would never do, let me remind you that everything we have is to be devoted to God. All our substance and everything we have has been loaned to us by God. All that we have and all that we are is because of him. We must be faithful to give it all back to him.

LET'S PRAY

Lord Jesus, you have given me every spiritual blessing in the heavenly realm. I have it all, and I thank you for your gracious gifts to me. I want to live in the light of your Word. Help me to honor you with every treasure you have given to me. I want my life to magnify you today. Take me. Take my life, my treasure, my talents, and use them for your glory. Amen.

26

OUR ACTIONS AFFECT OTHERS

One sinner destroys much good.

ECCLESIASTES 9:18 NIV

In that way, whatever happens to one member happens to all. If one suffers, everyone suffers. If one is honored, everyone rejoices.

1 CORINTHIANS 12:26

Achan's sin affected more than just his own life. His sin brought the whole camp into a curse. This is reminiscent of Abraham's disobedience in Egypt, which almost cost him his wife. Abraham was willing to surrender his wife but not his life. We also see a parallel in David's disobedience in taking the unauthorized census, which led to the death of seventy thousand people. Our actions and the decisions we make can seriously alter the lives of others. Do we realize the damage and destruction that one corrupt, compromising life can bring into the camp and household of God?

Sin was defiling the entire camp of the Israelites. So, it wasn't just about Achan; God was also dealing with all his people. You see, God deals with us as a body, as a whole. We're all one; all are blessed together, and all suffer together. We are the body of Christ, and we belong to each other. We need each other, and we affect each other. Any weakness or infection in one part of your physical body affects your entire body, and so it is in the body of Christ. It wasn't just Achan hiding his stolen items; it was the entire camp of Israel that was accountable for sin before God. Isn't that amazing how God sees the unity of the body? And we have to see it as he does.

THE GENEALOGY OF SIN

In Achan's confession, he said three simple statements. He said, "I saw...I wanted...I took." He described how he saw the Babylonian garment, the silver, and the golden wedge. He saw them, and he wanted them. He let that lust into his soul and then crossed the line and took them. "I saw, I wanted, I took" is the genealogy of his sin. The same can happen to us; our eyes gaze on something, it stirs up a desire inside of us, and we begin to want what we see. Whether it's lust, materialism, or the longing for honor that comes when we watch someone else being esteemed and not us, these things can take an illegitimate hold on our heart.

> For all that the world can offer us—the gratification of our flesh, the allurement of the things of the world, and the obsession with status and importance—none of these things come from the Father but from the world. (1 John 2:16)

HIDING OUR SIN

Achan's mistake was to think that he could get away with sin simply by hiding the loot. God spoke to Joshua during this exposure of Achan's sin and told Joshua he was not only to put to death the man caught with the devoted things but also "everything that man owns you must likewise destroy by fire, for he has violated the covenant of YAHWEH" (Joshua 7:15). You see, Achan had goats, sheep, and livestock. He was actually a man of great wealth. Yet he took things that were not his. He didn't need them; he simply wanted them.

> Then Joshua, and all of Israel with him, took Achan son of Zerah along with the silver, the robe, the bar of gold, and all that belonged to him—his sons, daughters, donkeys, oxen, sheep, tent—everything. Joshua led them all to the Valley of Trouble [Achor] and said, "Why have you brought all this trouble on us? YAHWEH will bring trouble on you today!" (vv. 24–25)

The names Achan and Valley of Achor are a play on words. Achan, you have brought "Achan" to the people of God; now the Lord is going to bring you to "Achor," the Valley of Trouble.

> Then all the people stoned Achan and his family to death. They burned up the bodies and all Achan's possessions. They raised over him a huge mound of stones that remains to this day. That is why the place was called the Valley of Trouble ever since. (vv. 25–26)

This pile of rocks was like a memorial. It was as an altar where sin was dealt with and compromise was put out of the camp. This was a necessary step on the path to possessing their inherited promised land. And so it is with you and me. Before we can possess our promised inheritance, we must walk free of all compromise. Then we can go on into the land of glory that God has given us, everything God has destined for us to possess. It's time to confess and come clean. It's time to walk through the gateway of hope.

A Gateway of Hope

God ends this tragic story of Achan with a precious promise. As was mentioned before, Achan and Achor are both translated "trouble," as it's the same Hebrew root word. That place has been called the "Valley of Trouble" ever since that fateful day. But centuries later, a prophet named Hosea prophesied a full-circle promise that brings forth the message of God's redemptive heart for us and our troubles.

Hosea has a very unique story. As a prophetic act, he married a prostitute. He bound his heart to a damaged, unholy bride and made a covenant with her. This is symbolic of our relationship with God. He is faithful even when we are not. Hosea then took this message of hope to another level by prophesying, "I…will make the Valley of Achor a door of hope" (Hosea 2:15 NIV).

God's promise is this: *If my people will deal with compromise, a door of hope will be opened to you. And I will take that messed up, horrible ditch you fell into, that place of trouble and pain, and you will pass through into hope.* You can move from that realm of destruction through the doorway of hope that God has promised to you. You are not without hope, my friend! A gateway of hope has been opened to us, and we can pass through and bring other people there to rest as well. Even the Valley of Trouble will be transformed into a gateway of hope. Hallelujah!

Let's Pray

Lord, open the eyes of my heart to see that there's not a compromise or sin in me that you cannot redeem when I confess. I thank you as your new-covenant believer that I now live in the day where the gateway of hope has been opened up to me and I can pass through. Thank you for your Holy Spirit, who brings conviction and leads me to the mercy seat, to the place of surrender, and on through the gateway of hope. I love you, Lord, and surrender all to you as my resting place. In Jesus' name. Amen.

27

GRACE OVERCOMES

Joshua was a city-reacher, a true leader. Leaders in this Joshua generation will lead God's people into their inheritance. They will take God at his word and believe in a regional impact of the gospel. Cities will be taken for Christ in the days to come. The Joshua generation will believe they can have what they ask for, and they won't quit until they move the church into her destiny.

Not only was Joshua godly, but he was also bold. However, his confidence did not spring from some choleric "type A" personality but rather from his intimate encounters with God. Joshua's confidence came from being in the dwelling place in the tent of Moses. Long after Moses left, the young man Joshua stayed there in the burning presence. No wonder he and Caleb had the spirit of faith to look at the intimidating giant population of Canaan and still know that God would win the day. And today God is raising up a Joshua generation that operates in the Holy Spirit of faith and bold confidence, knowing that everything God has promised in the book, God can accomplish through them. They will press though until they lay hold of their inheritance in God.

FAILURE BECOMES A VICTORY

In Joshua 8, Joshua brings the people of God back to Ai. This time they have a different perspective, and they want God's strategy. As we see in the beginning of the chapter, he gives them a truly incredible plan, but before he does, he encourages them with this message:

> YAHWEH said to Joshua, "Do not yield to fear nor shrink back because of Israel's failure." (v. 1)

The words *shrink back* in Hebrew mean "broken down." If there is any word in the Hebrew that would come close to the meaning of a nervous breakdown, it would be the words *shrink back* right here in Joshua 8. So, just listen to the heart of God for his people. No matter what you have done or been through, he's saying, *Don't have a nervous breakdown over your failure. I'm going to give you another chance. Don't be broken down by your past shame. Don't be knocked down into the dust, where you can't get back up and claim the victory and take the promised land. I am still with you. Victory is waiting for you!*

THE "ALL" PRINCIPLE

> Now get up, take all your soldiers with you, and march against Ai. See, I have handed over to you the city, the king, his people, and his land. Do to Ai what you did to Jericho and its king, except this time, you may take the plunder, including livestock. Set an ambush behind the city. (Joshua 8:1–2)

God tells Joshua to take *all* the army. In the Hebrew text, the word *all, entire,* or *whole* occurs twenty-one times in this chapter. God was really making a point! In fact, the key to understanding this chapter of Joshua is the word *all.* God wants all. He wants all of the people to go in and conquer all of the city and bring all of the glory back to him.

He also gave them some very comforting words. He told Joshua to go and attack Ai, for "I have handed over to you the city, the king, his people, and his land." Friend, God has already done it! He has done it and won it. Our victory is secured as long as we are with and in him.

Remember, *Ai* means "a heap of ruins." This is a picture of this world system with the compromises, the mess-ups of our life that have become a heap of ruins. God doesn't want us to sweep it all under a religious rug, but he wants us to face our disgraces. The "Ai" in your life has to be conquered. He says, "Do to Ai what you did to Jericho…except this time you may take the plunder." You will get your redemption and a reward.

THE GRACE FACTOR

I'm just so impressed with God's grace! It may be hard to believe, but God delights to give us second chances. You may be saying right now, "I have miserably failed. I've done something that I am so ashamed of. All is lost!" Well, do you know what the Word of God says? It says that God always has a redemptive plan. He is so much greater than any of our failures. He is the Savior of our second chances.

> When YAHWEH delights in how you live your life,
> he establishes your every step.
> If they stumble badly, they will still survive,

129

for the Lord lifts them up with his hands.
(Psalm 37:23–24)

The secret to success in life is knowing God's grace. When we fail, we must get back up. By grace we are assured that our heavenly Father is still there for us. He won't give up on you. He won't shake his head in disgust and walk away. He keeps going after you, reaching for your heart to lift you up and to give you that change. When the Lord saves us, he takes into consideration all of our tumbles and stumbles. He knows we're going to still have all the mess-ups, and yet he still takes us into his family. Listen, if God is omniscient (and he is), then he knows ahead of time that we're going to fail him. He knows we'll offend some people and that, sadly, we will be a source of pain to somebody in the future. And yet, God still brings us into his embrace and says, *Come to me, my beloved. It's all going to be okay. My grace is sufficient. As your day is, so will your strength be. If you fall, I will pick you up because I have made you righteous in my sight, and I call you good in my eyes.*

So, Joshua took his entire army and fought against Ai. We learn these two vital lessons from this portion of Joshua: (1) We need to connect with the entire body of Christ to see a city reached for the gospel. (2) Failure is never final because of the grace of God. And we'll talk more about this in the next chapter.

LET'S PRAY

Lord Jesus, I'm learning each day that I have nothing except your grace. You are my strength and my life. Help me in every challenge I face this day to lean upon you, my Beloved. Your Word is enough for me, and your Spirit will guide me from one victory to the next. In Jesus' name. Amen.

28

LAUNCH INTO YOUR NEW DAY

How would you like a divine do-over in Jesus Christ? How would you like to start all over again with a clean slate? That is what Calvary means for us. It's important, then, that every one of us just freely launches out by faith into a brand-new beginning.

I love those Etch A Sketch toys we played with as children, don't you? Life is like that. Life with God is like an Etch A Sketch. You're going along, trying to make something good of your life. You're trying to get it right. Then you blow it on the Etch A Sketch of your life. Despite all your good intentions, things go horribly bad. You never meant to make that mistake. You never wanted that marred picture, yet here you are, looking at your "heap of ruins." But the good thing about an Etch A Sketch is that after a good shaking, you have a clean slate. You can start all over.

Maybe that's you. You need a new day. New days bring new mercies, new strengths, new opportunities to soar into what God is doing. Today is not what he did yesterday. So, do what you need to do to make things right, and God will help you rise out of your days of past failures. And then forget them and move forward. Forget the former things in order to embrace the new. "I forget all of the past as I fasten my heart to the future instead" (Philippians 3:13).

Fasten your heart to the future. Press on into the new day. Move forward, never looking back. That's how Jesus wants us to live. I just want to put my heart toward heaven and forget about the rest. Let's lay all of our life's messes at the foot of the cross. His scandalous grace qualifies the unqualified for a brand-new beginning. Reach out by faith today and take your new beginning.

A NEW STRATEGY

Joshua and his entire army set out to attack Ai. He chose thirty thousand valiant warriors and sent them ahead by night with these instructions: "Now pay attention. Set an ambush behind Ai, but don't hide very far away. Stay alert and ready for battle! I'll lead the rest of the army and make a direct assault on the city, and when they come out to fight us, we'll flee from them as we did the first time. When this happens, they'll say to themselves, 'Look! They're running away from us, just like last time!' And they'll keep chasing us until we've lured them away from the city. While we're running away from them, jump up from your hiding place, race into Ai, and seize it. YAHWEH, your God, will deliver the city into your hands! When you've captured the city, set

> it on fire. Now that you have your orders, go and do
> as YAHWEH has commanded!" (Joshua 8:3–8)

This Israelite army was to run up to make an assault on the city and then run away. Of course, all of the people of Ai would then chase after the Israelites, who would be pretending to run away in fear. It kind of looked like a game of tag. You're it! But Joshua, by the wisdom of God, put five thousand men behind the city as an ambush. "He placed a smaller force of about five thousand men west of the city to set an ambush between Bethel and Ai" (v. 12).

So Joshua sends the five thousand ambushers around the back of the city to hide until he signals them. Then twenty-five thousand soldiers come up to the walls of Ai, put on the most fearful act that they could muster, and then they run away from the Ai army. It was a trap!

THE GOD OF INFINITE VARIETY

You see, God is not only the God of new beginnings; he's the God of infinite variety and creativity. God's strategies are unique. He didn't tell the Israelites to do the same thing they did at Jericho. This was a brand-new city-reaching strategy. God is looking for men and women who will trust him for the tailor-made strategy he creates to win their unique spiritual battles. There are principles in the Word that will always work, but there are also those strategies that come straight from the throne room of God that you will have to find for your particular issues. We are so blessed that he welcomes us into his throne of grace to find what we need when we need it.

> So now we draw near freely and boldly to where
> grace is enthroned, to receive mercy's kiss and dis-
> cover the grace we urgently need to strengthen us
> in our time of weakness. (Hebrews 4:16)

> If anyone longs to be wise, ask God for wisdom
> and he will give it! He won't see your lack of wis-
> dom as an opportunity to scold you over your
> failures but he will overwhelm your failures with
> his generous grace. (James [Jacob] 1:5)

Yes, indeed, God is the God of infinite variety. His heavenly wisdom and empowering grace are only "a prayer away." New, unique, and varied strategies will open to us if we but ask him. As the old hymn "I Must Tell Jesus" says, "If I but ask Him, He will deliver. Make of my troubles, quickly an end!"[14]

Jericho's strategy was quite different from Ai's, and that's an understatement! At Jericho, the Israelite army spent a week marching in broad daylight, but the attack on Ai was covert, and their covert "op" prepared the way for the daylight assault to come. At Jericho, the whole army remained united, but Joshua *divided* the army for the attack on Ai. You see, just because you got a victory in your life last week and God did something really cool, that doesn't mean that he's going to pull that same "trick out of the hat" again for you this week. The wisdom for us in this story is that we are going to have to seek him continually for his strategy, for his wisdom, and for his fresh revelation. It's not a formula. It's a friendship, our relationship, and it always will be.

It's important that we seek God's will for every spiritual battle that stands in front of us. God will always organize victory out of our mistakes if we'll seek him and follow his instructions. He will lead us from victory to victory. And he will lead us from our defeat to victory when we've failed to follow him. Thank you, Lord, for not giving up on us! In the next chapter we will find out how this divine strategy worked for the Joshua generation.

LET'S PRAY

Lord, so many times in my day I need your wisdom. Shine a light on my heart and give me living understanding so that I choose the right path, speak the right words, and do the right things. I ask you for your wisdom, and I want your wisdom to be demonstrated in my life and my relationships. Guard my heart in your love. I pray in Jesus' name. Amen.

29

VICTORY AT AI

At dawn, when the king of Ai saw the Israelites, he and his army rushed out to fight. They ran to attack Israel at a predetermined place...not knowing that an ambush had been set against them behind the city. Joshua and all the main fighting force fled toward the wilderness as though they were being overcome. Joshua's tactic drew all of Ai's reinforcements out of the city, and they set off in hot pursuit of Joshua and his men. Not a man remained in Ai or in Bethel who did not go out in pursuit of Israel, leaving their city undefended.

JOSHUA 8:14–17

At dawn, the king of Ai saw the entire Hebrew army positioned in front of the city. Confident of victory, they emptied out the city to attack Israel. But God had situated Joshua and his army for victory. This time they were not relying on themselves and their wisdom, but they positioned themselves according to God's instructions ahead of time. It's the same way for us. When we place ourselves in the strategies of heaven, the strongholds of the enemy will be broken and defeated. Not only that, but we will inherit the spoils of victory as well.

> Then Yahweh spoke to Joshua and said, "Now, take the spear in your hand and point it toward Ai, for I will hand the city over to you!" So Joshua pointed his spear toward the city, and when Joshua gave this signal, all the men waiting in ambush behind the city jumped up from their position and poured into Ai. They quickly captured it and set it on fire. (Joshua 8:18–19)

God told Joshua to lift up his spear. It was almost like Moses lifting up the rod against the Amalekites (see Exodus 17:8–13). Joshua lifted up his spear as a signal to the warriors, and the men hidden behind the city raced in and set it on fire.

Holy Smoke!

> When the men of Ai looked back, they saw the smoke of their city rising to the sky. Joshua and his men also saw the smoke and knew that the other Israelite soldiers had captured the city and had set it on fire. The army of Ai had no place to escape, so Joshua and his men turned on them and began killing them. (Joshua 8:20–21)

Ai's army was destroyed. The whole city of Ai was destroyed. And it says that when Joshua's army saw the smoke, they turned around and fought. This story is an incredible picture of how God wants you to win your battle. He wants you to take the stronghold of oppression that has come against you (and which perhaps has even brought a defeat into your life) and turn it all around. When you see the smoke of the glory of God's finished sacrifice, you know that the victory is won.

Friend, you need to see the smoke. You need to see where God has set the seal of the sacrifice of the finished work. When the army of God saw the smoke rising over the city, they knew that the sacrifice had been made and that the victory was theirs. They ran into the city, pursued their enemies, cut them down—leaving neither survivors nor fugitives—and took all of the spoils. We need to see the smoke over every stronghold of the enemy.

A Heap of Ruins and a Heap of Stones

> Then Joshua burned Ai to the ground and reduced it to a mound of ruins for all time. It remains desolate to this day. And he hanged the king of Ai on a tree until sunset. Then at sunset, Joshua had the corpse taken down and left it lying in front of where the city gates once stood. They raised a large pile of stones over his corpse, where it remains to this day. (Joshua 8:28–29)

The king over a heap of ruins is now under a heap of stones. As previously mentioned, Ai means "heap of ruins." It's a picture of the world system. God's warriors went out of Bethel and conquered Ai. *Bethel* means "the house of God." It's from out of the house of God that we plunder the heap of ruins. Ai's men were twelve thousand. Twelve is the number of the apostolic government. This is a picture of ruling. The destruction of Ai portrays the utter defeat of the rulership of this world system. That is what we must throw off. This all speaks to us as God's people, his army, the Joshua generation, rising up and conquering the strongholds that keep the church from moving into the fullness of God's government. We must arise and dismantle this world's system of darkness.

ADAM HANGED ON A TREE

Ai's king was hanged on a tree. Who's the king of this world system? Where did all this sin problem come from? It came from a man named Adam. Ai's king, the one who led this whole debacle, was Adam. The "Adam" in you was hanged on a tree. This is a picture of our co-crucifixion with Christ. And Ai represents this world system with its strongholds. It has its twelve thousand–strong army trying to govern and impress the authorities and the kingdom of darkness. It endeavors to enslave us with its lies. But when we see the sacrifice of Christ and his holy smoke rising up to proclaim Christ's victory, it's all over for the enemy. And it's from out of Bethel, "the house of God," that we go and conquer.

> Then Jesus made a public spectacle of all the powers and principalities of darkness, stripping away from them every weapon and all their spiritual authority and power to accuse us. And by the power of the cross, Jesus led them around as prisoners in a procession of triumph. He was not their prisoner; they were his! (Colossians 2:15)

A NEW COMMITMENT

It's time for a new commitment. How badly do you want it? How much do you want your new day and your promised inheritance? Radical love and passion will produce radical obedience.

Passion will push you to purity. If you really want everything God has for you, you can go get it. He is not withholding anything good from you. In fact, it's already been provided for you!

> God has proved his love by giving us his greatest treasure, the gift of his Son. And since God freely offered him up as the sacrifice for us all, he certainly won't withhold from us anything else he has to give. (Romans 8:32)

So, they took Ai's king (our old nature), put him on a tree (the cross), and buried his body under a heap of stones as a memorial to show that God had won the victory. This is the way it must be with our old way of life. There has to be a witness, a memorial stone, that shows that we have been crucified with Christ and that the life that we now lead is his, and then we are ready to step into our new commitment to walking in his continuous victory.

LET'S PRAY

God, your ways are beyond my understanding. The way you bring me to victory is amazing! I am in awe of your power and grace operating in my life. I praise you, Father. Keep working in my life today and bring me into a new victory—a victory that will bring glory to you alone. Amen.

30

Spiritual Warfare

Now when all the kings west of the Jordan heard about these things—those in the hill country in the western foothills, and along the entire coast of the Great Sea as far as Lebanon (the kings of the Hittites, Amorites, Canaanites, Perizzites, Hivites, and Jebusites)— they came together to make war against Joshua and Israel.

Joshua 9:1-2

Jesus, our heavenly Joshua, is going to take the promised land within you. As Joshua fought battles to possess the land of Israel, so Jesus will fight your battles to drive out every enemy that you're allowing to reside in your heart. This is where spiritual warfare begins...not in the heavenlies but in the "heartlies!" Let's talk about those eight "-ites" that were living in God's promised land. Each one of them is significant and represents distinct spiritual combatants you must overcome in your journey to fullness.

THE HITTITES

The word *Hittite* in the Hebrew means "to be broken in pieces," "terror," or "dread." The Hittites are spiritual terrorists. They utilize fear, dread, revenge, and retaliation in order to defeat you. This manifests with a strong sense of self-protection, which says, "Don't cross me. Don't bug me. Give me my space." This "Hittite" attitude is an angry influence that will attempt to break you to pieces and throw you into fits of rage. With Christ, we own the victory, and it's time to say, "No deal! For Christ is my protector." If he is going to take you fully to be his inheritance, the Hittites cannot be allowed to roam around in a land that's already been conquered by the one who has conquered all.

THE AMORITES

The word *Amorites* in the Hebrew means "highlanders" or "summit dwellers." It's a picture of pride, arrogance, elitism, and superiority. It is a spirit that keeps us from the fresh brokenness and humility that God wants to bring into our hearts so we can connect with him in deeper intimacy. You know, pride is one of the grossest forms of deception and self-worship. It basically says, *God is working only in me.* It deludes us into thinking that we're the only ones God is using. It says, *I have the mind of the Lord, and therefore, you don't. I am a "highlander." I am a "summit dweller." I am the "top dog."* But the Lord draws near to those who have entered the low and broken place. He is near the contrite of heart and remains distant from the proud (see Psalm 138:6). The high and lofty one can be found by the low, broken, and humble of heart. Isn't that true? Jesus is the Most High, and yet he completely humbled himself to save us. If God so humbled himself, can't we? This truly is the path to peace and blessing, so we must kick out the Amorite attitude.

THE CANAANITES

The word *Canaanite* means "merchants," "pirates," or "traffickers." They represent materialism, the love of money, and the worship of mammon. Materialism is a god-like spirit. It's a demonic power that is gripping many in the church today. This Canaanite has to be cast out. Just as Joshua's commission was to conquer the Canaanites, we, too, must put the love of money under our feet. It is a root of all evil (see 1 Timothy 6:10). It can be a wellspring of bitter waters that pollute and defile. It can blind us to the kingdom purposes of God. When we set our hearts on riches, we are actually chasing vanity, and how quickly it flies from us. Worthless distractions will keep us from pursuing what truly matters most—Christ and his kingdom. When you know that God is your provider, you will not err by chasing materialism.

THE PERIZZITES

The name of the Perizzites is taken from a Hebrew word that means "rustic country dwellers" or "country folk." The Perizzites in us speak of lacking vision, being stuck in tradition, and being inordinately loyal to the old rusty ways. It represents being "locked in" to our own territory and spiritual domain. Perizzites love to keep us looking back to the old instead of forward to the new. If you are so comfortable in your tradition that you won't launch out into a realm of faith and trust with God alone, then you may be bowing to this spirit. The Perizzite attitude needs to be driven out. In essence, it is the fear of change, the lack of vision, and the inability to move into the promises of God because we fear what others will say. It is time to come out of that restraining fear of the unknown and come into the anointing of the Holy Spirit, where freedom and boldness resolutely drive out all fear of men, all lack of vision, and all love of the traditions of the old rusty and crusty ways of the past.

THE HIVITES

Most Jewish commentators believe the word *Hivite* is taken from the Chaldean word for "serpent." However, other etymologists believe the meaning is from a word that means "to lay out in order." The enemy of our soul is always laying out a trap for us. The Hivites point to the schemes of the enemy to hinder your advance into fully possessing your spiritual inheritance. Every plan the enemy has will be thwarted as we see ourselves in Christ and apply the power of God's Word to our lives.

THE JEBUSITES

The word *Jebusite* in Hebrew means "trodden down," "conquered," or "subdued." It's a picture of depression, fear, panic, and anxieties that weigh and oppress the human soul. It's the habit of walking in discouragement rather than in divine optimism and the spirit-inspired revelation that God has already won for us. We must hold to the truth in our hearts that God's vision for the future is hope. It's always what he spells out for us. People can tell all the judgment stories and doomsday prophecies they want to of how the earth is going to quake and the nations are going to crumble, but I've read the Book, and I know the end of the story is hope. No matter what is going on in the world, God still reigns, and there is always hope (see Jeremiah 29:11). That's his long-range blueprint, and he is sticking to it, so let's kick out the Jebusite thinking from our land and get a vision of hope for the future.

THE GIRGASHITES

The Hebrew word for *Girgashite* (see Joshua 3:10) is taken from the word that means "dense." It speaks of a spirit of dullness, dullness of hearing, and ignorance. Some of us, at times, are just dense in our spiritual senses. We become spiritually dull of hearing and inept at moving at the sound of God's voice. Have you ever been there? I know I have. God, at times, has to "turn the volume up" in order for us to grasp and move with what he's saying to us. We must not be complacent or content with any Girgashites in our life. I believe sometimes we may fall into the trap of believing the lie that we aren't as spiritually "in tune" as others seem to be. This is simply not true! We are hardwired by the Almighty to hear his voice and communicate freely with him. God knows no other pattern of relationship than communion and communication—this is truly what you were created for. Don't settle for anything less; don't partner with the Girgashites.

THE GIBEONITES

The Gibeonites (see Joshua 9:9) speak of those who live in the hills, the high places, and the demonic strongholds. They are a picture of deceit, deception, and the demonic powers that rule in the high places. The Gibeonites represent cooperation with and adherence to the lies of spiritual powers that are not of God. This is where all of our troubles began: with the serpent in the garden. He was able to deceive Eve, and the rest is history. But Jesus came as the way, the truth, and the light. We no longer have to walk in deception. We'll learn more about the devious ways of our spiritual enemies, the Gibeonites, in the next chapter.

LET'S PRAY

Thank you, Lord, that you have created me for triumph. It's for conquering that I have been born again. Show me today how big and mighty you really are. I thank you, Jesus, that the victory is already won. You have blotted out my sins and given me the double cure of Calvary's love: I am forgiven of my sins and am unplugged from sin's power. The cross has made me free! Help me to fully step into the new beginning of that glorious future you have waiting for me. In Jesus' name. Amen.

31

DON'T BE DECEIVED

When the inhabitants of Gibeon learned how Joshua had destroyed Jericho and Ai, they resorted to a ruse: They sent a delegation disguised as messengers from a distant land. They loaded their donkeys with worn-out sacks and old, patched wineskins. They wore old, patched sandals on their feet and old, tattered clothes, and took along dry, moldy bread. When they arrived at Israel's camp at Gilgal, they said to Joshua and the Israelites: "We've come from a far country to propose that you make a treaty with us."

JOSHUA 9:3–6

The Joshua generation that God is raising up is a determined people who will not fall short of their inheritance but who know how to rest in his promises and push past every deceptive or demonic obstacle to possess those promises. Part of an

147

overcoming mentality is having a passionate determination to "make no treaty" with the enemy.

Make No Treaty with Darkness

Joshua made the mistake of not asking God about the Gibeonites. He failed to inquire of the Lord before agreeing to a treaty. Perhaps the victory over Jericho and Ai had left Joshua convinced that they would never again fail. Remember this lesson: after every victory will be a test. Joshua failed this test. He noticed the Gibeonites were all wearing worn-out clothes. They looked dusty from their seemingly long journey. Their bread was moldy, their sandals were worn out, and their wineskins were cracked and tearing. They looked the part. Deceivers often do.

So, Joshua took the "bait"—hook, line, and sinker. He believed their sob story about coming from a distant land when the actual truth was that they had only traveled about twenty miles. What pretenders they were! It's the same way with the enemy of our souls. He wants to deceive and destroy us. He has three basic ways that he comes to attack us. He comes as the roaring lion, the deceiving serpent, and an angel of light.

The Roaring Lion

> Be well balanced and always alert, because your
> enemy, the devil, roams around incessantly, like
> a roaring lion looking for its prey to devour.
> (1 Peter 5:8)

The ones the devil devours are those who fail to let go of their anxieties, worries, and stress and leave them with God. We must be well-balanced and always alert because if we aren't, self-pity and worry put us right into the devil's territory. In this world, we're living as Christians in enemy territory, and there's a lion prowling about. And one of the ways he wants to destroy you is by threatening and intimidating you with his roar. He terrorizes with his roaring fear tactics to keep us small, quiet, and on the defense. We've all heard that roar before, and if we cower in fear because of it, we will never possess our promises.

The Deceiving Serpent

> Now the snake was the most cunning of all living beings that YAHWEH-God had made. He deviously asked the woman, "Did God really tell you, 'You must not eat fruit from any tree of the garden—?'" (Genesis 3:1)

Deception is the most effective tool in the devil's toolbox. Knowing the truth can get difficult because we're all in love with our own opinions. We're sure of our philosophy, our way of living, our understanding of the Scriptures, and so on. And this thinking can quickly cause us to fall into deception. At times, we can even use the Bible as a weapon against those who disagree with us, beating them up with the Scriptures. Now, does that sound like the Father's way? That's not the Bible! That's just an opinion attached to a Scripture verse. But when you release the revelation of the Word of God, love always comes forth, and compassion is released. Even in judgment, there's mercy. Pride-filled opinions never produce the fruit of love; they only lead to deception and death. "Now I'm afraid that just as Eve was deceived by the serpent's clever lies, your thoughts may be corrupted and you may lose your single-hearted devotion and pure love for Christ" (2 Corinthians 11:3).

The beguiling subtlety of the serpent can take you away from the pure and simple devotion to Jesus Christ. You see, anything that complicates your life and keeps you away from this simplicity of pure love and devotion to Christ is of the devil. It has the sulfur smell all over it.

THE ANGEL OF LIGHT

> Even Satan transforms himself to appear as an angel of light! (2 Corinthians 11:14)

This passage in 2 Corinthians talks of pseudo-apostles and teachers with spiritual powers masquerading as God's servants. The entire books of Second Peter and Jude are in our Bible to warn us of deception and deceiving spirits. John, the pastor of love, tells us quite firmly to beware of "the spirit of antichrist" that is already sent into the world (1 John 4:3). According to John, for two thousand years, the antichrist spirit has been hard at work pulling people into darkness, deception, secular humanism, and all the other "-isms" of worldly philosophies (see 2 John 7).

God wants to bring the piercing light of truth to the human soul, not merely the intellect. The door to the truth is the spirit within you yielded to God. When we align ourselves with the Holy Spirit, then our hearts become a door to true understanding. However, if our hearts are not surrendered to the Holy Spirit, we are deceived. Every one of us. So, a powerful prayer we need to pray is, *Lord, show me where I have believed a lie.* As God's conquering company, marked by the spirit of Joshua, we must be careful of the devouring lion, the deceiving serpent, and the angel of light. We are real warriors in a real battle, and we have a real enemy.

The Need for Discernment

Israel's greatest danger (and ours!) wasn't the confederation of these seven armies inhabiting their land. Their greatest problem was the deception of the Gibeonites, who entered their camp and deceived their leader Joshua along with all the princes of Israel. Gibeon was only about twenty miles away. Yet no one seemed to realize their lies and deception. How we need discernment in our day to know what is truth and what is a lie! As we partner with our heavenly Joshua, our fierce Commander of Angel Armies will conquer and subdue every "-ite" and every lie that stands in our way.

Let's look at some of the lies these Gibeonites told God's people. First of all, they said they were from a distant country when they were actually neighbors. Second, they lied about their clothing and their food. Third, they lied about their identity, saying they were on an important envoy with a peace mission. And fourth, they called themselves Israel's servants, saying, "We are willing to be your servants!" (Joshua 9:8). And by the time their deception was revealed, it was too late...all because no one stopped to inquire of the Lord.

Let's Pray

Father, you are my hiding place. You are the one who rescues and redeems my soul, even when I fall. Give me your wisdom and help me to always seek your face when I am confused or tested. Give me grace today to be delivered from every form of self-deception. Search my heart. Break off every lie of the enemy from my mind and soul. I yield myself to your cleansing mercy. Amen.

32

THE FIVE-FOLD DECEPTION

[The Gibeonites] loaded their donkeys with worn-out sacks and
old, patched wineskins. They wore old, patched sandals on their
feet and old, tattered clothes, and took along dry, moldy bread.

JOSHUA 9:4–5

How easily is the human heart deceived! We think of ourselves more highly than we should, and when we do, deception
is a trap laid in front of us. The greatest protection from deception is humility. When we trust God and refuse to lean upon our
own ideas, opinions, and understanding, then grace becomes a
protective shield around our heart. But when we are proud and
self-assured, we become easy prey to the devil's strategies.

FIVE OLD-ORDER MENTALITIES

Notice the deceptive tactics the Gibeonites used in order to trick Joshua into thinking they had come from a distant land. First, they utilized their worn-out sacks. The Bible says they had loaded their donkeys with worn-out baggage. Think of "worn-out" sacks as old, dead, dry, worn-out religion, full of lifeless prayers and the old rituals that you've been trying to keep year after year because you thought there was power in them. But our dead works have not brought increase; they've only added to our misery.

Aren't you glad God doesn't say, "Behold, I do an old thing!" Or "I make you old creatures in Christ." Or "My mercies are old every morning." No way! He has new mercies for us every morning (see Lamentations 3:22–23). They're higher than the heavens. And although there's nothing new under the sun, his mercies don't come from under the sun. They're out of this world—they come from the heavens! The word *new* is written on everything God does. It's written all over him. It's time to embrace the new. So, get rid of your old, worn-out sack.

Secondly, they had an old wineskin. The old wineskin represents the old heart that is legalistic and brittle. It doesn't flex or bend. It is an unteachable heart, unable to learn something new. Throwing out the old wineskins of legalism doesn't mean walking in compromise. But it does mean walking in real love—love for God and love for people. It's the one standard God holds us to, and we shouldn't ever compromise it. Get rid of the old wineskin. It's brittle; it's cracked. It's just going to leak or rip apart. You've had it too long. It's time for a new day and new heart that will embrace it. God wants to put something new in you, but dry and dead religion can't hold the new.

Your heart is the wineskin. People want to apply the concept of "wineskin" to church structures. Still, a church can have a messed-up governmental structure but good people who have good hearts, and God will still bless it. On the other hand, you can have the perfect structure and an old, cold, rotten heart, and God will not bless that. You can be sure that if God finds hearts of love and passion and willingness to follow him, he will work it all out. In time, he will give you the right structure. He knows how to build his church, so you don't need to worry about that. We just need to be sure that we offer up to him a fresh wineskin to be filled, and he will do the rest.

The third form of deception was the worn and patched sandals. This represents the old walk and walking in old things. No life change, no transformation. Like the Gibeonites, we are all too quick to say, "I'm okay. You're okay. It's all okay." But it's not okay if we're walking in the old ways of the flesh when Jesus has given us a new and living way. God wants us to kick off those old sandals. And he's saying, "You're on holy ground. You walk on ground that is sanctified in the burning presence of the Lord." There is nothing fresh in your walk when you're walking on the old, so step into your new shoes of faith and peace and joy for the journey! God has called you to a new walk in Christ. Out with the old, in with the new.

The fourth is old clothes, the old rags they wore. This speaks of the old works of the flesh and trying to do good. The Bible says our own righteousness is as filthy rags. Now, if God had said that all of our sins are filthy rags, we would heartily agree—*Yes, Lord, amen! All of my sins are filthy rags*. But God doesn't say that. He says that all our righteousness is filthy. That's a whole different revelation, isn't it?

God is saying, *Oh child, I have given you life, and with it came my righteousness. So put behind you all the striving and trying to manipulate your way. All your determination, your resolutions will fall flat. You don't have to strive or work it out. Just turn it all over to me, and I will work it out. In fact, I already have. Throw off your old garment. My righteousness looks so much better. I will shine in and through you as you rest your heart in me. I am your righteousness!*

The fifth form of deception is old bread. The Gibeonites were living off the old crusts instead of a fresh revelation from God. Why would we ever settle for that? What about feasting on the manna? What about living bread? God wants to feed us with, "What is it?" That's what *manna* means in the Hebrew. It was a mystery, a sign and wonder pointing to God's power and love. We need to step into the unknown with God and live in the wonder and awe of super-dependence on the one who does wonders. God wants to feed you on his mysterious supply of wonder, the supernatural, hidden manna of heaven. And the golden jar of manna was placed in the ark, the chest. The chest is also your chest, in your heart and your soul. You are God's treasure chest! The golden jar of manna is Christ in you, the hope of glory. There is a Golden One inside of you, and it's Jesus. He will give you hidden manna. He'll give you the true, life-giving sustenance; you don't have to settle for crusts and crumbs. Come to the Lord's table and have fresh bread today and forever, every day!

SIMPLE SURRENDER

The key word in Joshua 9 is *old*. Until we get rid of the old, we're not going to embrace the new. But it's a new day, a brand-new season in the spirit realm. There's grace for each of us to come out of the Gibeonite deception. Let Joshua's sword, God's Holy Word, pierce our soul, and we can be set free and step into the new.

The Gibeonites told Joshua, "We greatly feared for our lives" (v. 24). That's the essence or root of deception. They feared the discipline and exposure that truth brings.

Jesus said, "The person who loves his life and pampers himself will miss true life! But the one who detaches his life from this world and abandons himself to me, will find true life and enjoy it forever!" (John 12:25). Human nature flees any kind of pain. You see, we don't want to lose the appearance of being cool or correct. We don't want to lose the image of perfection. We don't like to appear to fail. If we refuse to let go of that fear and pride, we can be sure that God will arrange a time for us to blow it, and everybody will know it. There won't be any "bragimonies" in heaven, only humble and grateful *testimonies* of God's goodness. And, if we are totally honest, we will see that our testimony is mostly this: *God tested me. I failed that test, but he loved me anyway.*

It's so freeing to just get broken by the Lord. It's so much easier to fall on the rock and be broken than to be crushed when the rock falls on you. We can bow in surrender and get rid of any Gibeonite deception. No more highlanders, no more prideful, arrogant superiority. Each one of us must come to Christ at "street level" with a humble heart. That is the pathway into the freedom and blessing of the new day where your kingdom comes to earth.

LET'S PRAY

Lord, I choose to enter into your loving presence, into the realm where all deception is left outside and where hunger and passion for you drive out all darkness. I receive the cure for my wayward heart: you, King Jesus. I come into your chambers, and I lay my life at your feet in surrender and devoted love. Wash me of the old and fill me with the new. I'm your vessel, Lord, your wineskin. Please fill me with new wine. I'm your empty water pot. Please fill me with a fresh overflowing of your living waters. Thank you, Jesus. Amen.

33

Redeeming Failure

Joshua summoned the Gibeonites and asked them, "Why did you deceive us? You told us that you lived very far from us, but we now know for a fact that you live right here near us. Therefore,…you will live under a curse, and you will be condemned to perpetual servitude. You will serve the house of my God by cutting wood and carrying water for us."

They answered Joshua, "We…feared for our lives…Now we are at your mercy, so do with us what you consider right and proper."

So Joshua had mercy and saved them from being killed by the Israelites. That day, he made them woodcutters and water carriers to serve the community of Israel for the altar of Yahweh at his divinely chosen place.

Joshua 9:22–27

By God's grace, the Israelites made their mistake work for them. God also wants you to take your mistakes and make them work for you. Joshua enlisted the Gibeonites and rebuked them for their deception but assured them that he and the Israelites would not break their oath to protect them. Joshua gives us an example of how we can make our failures work for us. He had the Gibeonites serve them.

There is no failure that is final when our hearts are after God. He will use our failures to teach life lessons we would learn no other way. God has woven our failures and our breakthroughs into who we are. When you fail, make your failures work for you by surrendering them to God. God can redeem every area of deception in our lives if we surrender to him.

So, after making the hasty covenant with the deceitful Gibeonites, Israel chose to honor their word as well. They refused to kill the Gibeonites because they knew the power of covenant, and they chose instead to make the inhabitants of Gibeon the woodcutters and water carriers in the house of God.

COVENANT

God is into covenant. The Israelites kept their covenant with the Gibeonites for four hundred years, but King Saul broke the covenant, and God judged his people for putting the Gibeonites to death (see 2 Samuel 21). You see, that's how powerful covenant is. In the Western world, we are not a society that celebrates covenant (see Romans 1:31). We really aren't. Our westernized culture is not based on covenant. It's based on attorneys and reading the fine print. It's based on hooking you, holding you, and binding you to a contractual agreement, or else. The honor of a person's word and the covenant that we enter into by oath no longer matters for many in our day. Even marriage vows are easily broken and easily ignored, but God doesn't ignore covenant. Thank God that we're his covenant sons and daughters. We've been brought into the covenant of faith, the covenant of hope in the Lord Jesus. God will never change his mind about us. He doesn't cut us off and say, "You're no longer my kid." No! We are his covenant, blood-bought sons and daughters, sealed with the covenant of love. And that covenant will never be broken. God has promised.

> "Even if the mountains were to crumble and the
> hills disappear,
> my heart of steadfast, faithful love will never
> leave you,
> and my covenant of peace with you will never be
> shaken,"
> says Yahweh, whose love and compassion will
> never give up on you. (Isaiah 54:10)

THE GIBEONITE CITIES

> The Israelites set out at once, and on the third
> day, they came to their cities: Gibeon, Chephirah,
> Beeroth, and Kiriath Jearim. But the Israelites did
> not attack them because the leaders of the assem-
> bly had sworn an oath to them in the name of
> Yahweh, the God of Israel. (Joshua 9:17–18)

There are four Gibeonite cities mentioned in verse 17: Gibeon, Chephirah, Beeroth, and Kiriath Jearim. We have already talked about the meaning of Gibeon in Chapter 30, so now let's look into the meanings of the other three cities and learn the lesson their names teach us.

CHEPHIRAH

Chephirah means "covered" or "overlaid." This is the place where sin, deception, and demons hide. It's where everything is covered up and hidden. It speaks of the lies we believe. For example: *I'm no good, I'll never overcome that problem, God can't heal me, I can't be forgiven, There's something wrong with me, or I'm unlovable.*

People may have spoken these lies over you. Perhaps they didn't even realize what they had done, but those words have become curses that play over and over in your head. They might have said, *You're never going to change, You're so dysfunctional,* or *You are such a loser.* These lies become a stronghold if we believe them. They seep into our soul and become our "inner truth."

We have to replace these lies with the truth of God's Word and then not settle for less than his best. God is our life-giving strength every step of the way. He is our victory. Right now! To walk in relationship with him right now—in our pain, in our insecurity, in our dysfunction, in the mess of our life—that's victory. We turn it over to him and say, *I love you where I am, right where I am. I'm not going to wait until I get somewhere else.* That's victory! You win right there in that place of faith. And then the ultimate victory is in God's hands. He'll take care of it. He'll bring all things into conformity to his will.

Soon you will start to reflect Jesus. Your face will shine like Moses because you're looking with an unveiled face into the glory, and you just keep going year after year, year after year. He will lead you in one continual triumph, one victory after another one. As we rest in him, letting our roots go deep in his Word and his love, he changes us from the inside out. And, before we know it, the deceptive lies of Chephirah no longer hold sway over our soul.

BEEROTH

Beeroth is "the place of wells." Beeroth represents the place of bitter waters and resentment. You may remember a well in the Bible where Jesus came and turned bitter waters of resentment into wells of living water (see John 4). He turned one Canaanite woman's water from bitter to sweet.

A troubled woman who had been married five times was living with a man who was not her husband, yet she found the place of wells. Her bitter waters became sweet as she drank from the well of living water that Jesus gave to her. It was at this well that the woman met Jesus and had her life changed forever from one of bitterness to a well of living water bubbling up, over, and out. She was so changed that she ran back into her city and told everyone there about the man who knew everything about her. And she told them all about the living springs of water that she herself had just been filled with. She became the first city-reacher of many to come.

That's what happens when you get filled with living water. Your vessel can not contain it all. You have to pour it out on others.

KIRIATH JEARIM

Kiriath Jearim means "the place of dense thickets, overgrown." It represents the traditions of men, the rehashing of the theologies of man, and the vain traditions of religion. But our true victory that overcomes the world is our faith in the Lord Jesus. Not form and ritual.

Here's our problem: we don't like to give up our old, familiar customs. God is forever the Creator. He loves to create. Every day he renews us, re-creates us, and makes things new. He loves for us to sing a new song, and he calls us his new creation people.

It's time to leave the Gibeonite cities behind and walk into the new. Yes, the new will always bring a challenge, but the new is the only way we advance and move forward. Are you ready for whatever new thing God wants to do in your life?

LET'S PRAY

My Father, I love how you take my failures and redeem them and use them to change my life. I yield everything I am and everything I have to you. Take me forward into the new treasures of your love that you long to reveal to me. I'm ready to make a break with my past and launch into all that you have for me. Help me today as I take steps forward into your plan for my life. Amen.

34

OUTNUMBERED

The city of Gibeon was larger than Ai…and all its men were
known as great warriors. So King Adoni-zedek of Jerusalem sent
messages to King Hoham[15] of Hebron, King Piram of Jarmuth,[16]
King Japhia of Lachish,[17] and King Debir of Eglon:[18] "The people of
Gibeon have made peace with Joshua and the Israelites. Come and
help me attack them."
The five Amorite kings joined forces…Their combined armies
surrounded Gibeon and attacked it.
The Gibeonites sent out a call for help to Joshua at the camp in
Gilgal: "Don't abandon us, for we are your servants! Come quickly
and save us! Help us, for the Amorite kings of the hill country have
surrounded us!"[19] So Joshua and all his fighting men, all the mighty
warriors of Israel, left Gilgal to aid the Gibeonites.
YAHWEH spoke to Joshua: "Do not fear the Amorite kings and their
armies, for I have decreed your victory over them; not one will

withstand you!"
Joshua and his fighting force marched all night long from Gilgal to
Gibeon and took them all by surprise! Joshua inflicted a crushing
defeat on them at Gibeon, for YAHWEH threw the Amorites into a
panic at the sudden sight of Israel's army!

JOSHUA 10:1–10

Do you ever feel outnumbered, surrounded by many enemies? That must have been how Joshua felt. The armies of five kings now surrounded the city that Joshua entered into a covenant to protect. He had no choice. He must go and help others, even those who had once deceived him. This speaks loudly of the character of Joshua to go and intervene and fight enemies who outnumbered his forces. The armies of five kings, who were all mighty warriors, against Joshua and the Israelites. Maybe you can guess how this will turn out. God plus Joshua was enough.

It Is Time to Go on the Offensive

Joshua led his troops on a nine-hour, all-night march to Gibeon. It was a daring move. At dawn, the massive armies of the confederacy were shocked! There stood Joshua and his warriors, ready for battle. Joshua took them by surprise!

Some of us know nothing about battle except defense, but the Joshua generation will operate in a new orientation for spiritual battle. God wants to activate you and shift you from the defensive posture in spiritual warfare to being on the offense. Listen, you have what it takes to win every battle because the Victorious One dwells in you. So, rise up! Shake off all fear and passivity. Declare today, "I'm not going to take it anymore. Christ has won the victory, and I am stepping in by faith to claim what he has already done!" There is a phrase that describes the condition of those who are passive and refuse to go on the offense. It's called living in defeat. But the Lord didn't call you to a life of passivity and defeat; he called you to a life of victory.

Defeat doesn't come when the attack begins. It comes the moment we choose to be passive or when we give in. When passivity takes over our hearts, the next thing we know, we'll become a spiritual punching bag for the enemy. We've all faced it, but we can't remain there. If we do, we'll find that we'll never walk into our inheritance, our promises, our destiny.

The one who spoke the world into existence and has all power and authority stands with us in every demonic standoff. And because of the blood of Christ, we can walk in the confidence and the boldness that Jesus has secured for us. We can stand and face any giant, no matter the disparity in size, strength, ability, or influence. In the natural, I may be weak and small, but there's a full-grown, mighty Jesus roaring with power and anointing on the inside of me. If we will lift our thoughts from ourselves and our ability to fight in the natural and we begin to appropriate the Word of God (our armor) and stand on what's already been done for us in faith, we win! Our rescuer has already gone into the battle before us, and he is our mighty Defender, the Commander of Angel Armies. David was a fierce warrior, and he knew and trusted in the source of his strength, God alone: "With you [Lord] as my strength I can crush an enemy horde, advancing through every stronghold that stands in front of me" (Psalm 18:29).

Advancing! That is our faith stance. Can you see it? This fearless "bring it on!" attitude is what we as the church must step into. We are fully covered, fully equipped, and fully loved. And, just like David and Joshua, we already have the victory. God doesn't teach us to run and hide. No, the Bible says to resist the devil, and he will flee. It is time to watch the enemy run.

LEAVE THE PITY PARTY

It's time to leave self-pity behind. Self-pity is the devil's babysitter. It's the daycare of demonic powers. Many Christian soldiers have relinquished their weapons and armor in order to shrink back passively to that "safe place," which really isn't a safe place. It's false comfort. We may get momentary relief from the pressures of the fight, but we are only making a trade-off, where we're headed for a far greater defeat in the future. We will never possess our inheritance if we play nice with the devil. Never. In fact, we should never play with the devil.

Here's the truth: you're not any less blessed than Jesus. So, let me ask you, is Jesus defeated, worried, or nervous? No way! He's actually sitting in the heavens laughing for joy. Well then, why can't we laugh? If we'll get back up there into the heavenly places (our dwelling place) where we're meant to be, we'll begin to see every struggle the way he sees it. Then we can laugh too. It's time to get a different perspective of spiritual warfare. Let's receive a new upgrade with the strategy of a more-than-a-conqueror!

The choice is ours for how long we remain in the passivity pit. We can stay in the devil's pity party for another decade if we want to, but somewhere in our journey, we will have to declare these words in order for us to possess our full inheritance in God. Like the Shulamite when she faces the dark night of her soul, we must finally declare, "I will get up now and go…search for the one my heart loves" (Song of Songs 3:2 NIV). I will leave behind the heaviness of discouragement, and I will rise up!

LET'S PRAY

Almighty God, I hide myself in you. Your strength, your might are enough for me. I will shake off the discouragement of my past and embrace the power of your life in me today. Nothing can stop me when I trust in you. Help me to make good choices. I choose to rest in you even when I feel like I'm surrounded by my enemies. Come, Lord Jesus, and be my strength today. Amen.

35

THE DAY THE SUN STOOD STILL

[Joshua's warriors] slaughtered the kings' armies all the way to Azekah and the city of Makkedah. As the Amorites raced down the hill to Beth Horon, Yahweh hurled large hailstones on them from the sky! The hail continued to fall all the way to Azekah; in fact, more men died from Yahweh's hailstones than by the swords of the Israelites.

Yahweh gave the men of Israel victory over the Amorites that day, the day when Joshua stood before the people and prayed to Yahweh:

"Sun, stand still over Gibeon!

Moon, stay where you are over the valley of Aijalon!"[20]

And so the sun stood still in the middle of the sky and was in no hurry to set until one day became two. And the moon halted while

the nation triumphed over its enemies—as it is also recorded in the
Scroll of the Upright One.[21] It was the day YAHWEH himself fought
for Israel! There has never been a day like it before or since—a day
when YAHWEH obeyed the voice of a man!

JOSHUA 10:10–14

The fiercest battle that Joshua ever faced is recorded for us here in Joshua 10. After the victories of Jericho and Ai, he and his band of warriors came up against an overwhelming confederacy of Canaanite kings. There is strength in numbers, and this was certainly an intimidating response to Joshua's advance into the promised land. However, even in their vast numbers, these kings didn't stand a chance before the living God. Joshua, empowered by the Lord, beat a path of victory through the land of Canaan, dividing and conquering as he went. In the exact same way, God will lead us from victory to victory, no matter how great the odds may be stacked against us—because with God, all things are possible.

Did you notice it? YAHWEH himself fought alongside Israel. God supernaturally directed the hailstones to hit the Amorites but not the Israelites (see Psalm 91:7). There have been reports in human history of record hailstones weighing over 120 pounds. The largest hailstone in recent US history fell in South Dakota and was nearly the size of a volleyball. Hail is a biblical symbol of God's truth and justice that destroys the refuge (web) of lies (see Exodus 9:18–35; Isaiah 28:17; Revelation 11:19).

This chapter of Joshua contains perhaps one of the most amazing miracles recorded in Israel's history. By the decree of a mortal, the entire cosmos paused as YAHWEH himself fought for his people. Can you imagine what that was like? God stopped the cosmic order because of a man's decree! "Sun, stand still...Moon, stay where you are!" What power was released in the universe as the cycle of the sun and moon went on pause. Joshua stopped the sun!

God will go to any length to see you win your battles as you live in faith and obedience to him. God is the engineer of the universe and holds its controls in his hands. He can accelerate or slow down the created order he set in place. Never underestimate the power of your prayer. When your prayer becomes a decree, heaven will respond. YAHWEH obeyed the voice of a man.

JOSHUA CAPTURES THE FIVE KINGS

When Joshua was told that the five kings had been found hiding in a cave at Makkedah, Joshua ordered his men, "Seal up the mouth of the cave with large stones and post guards in front of it. But don't stop! Pursue your enemies! Cut off their retreat and don't let them reach their cities, for YAHWEH your God has given them into your hand!"

So Joshua and the Israelites nearly killed them all—almost to a man—although a few escaped into the fortified cities. The whole army returned safely to Joshua at the camp in Makkedah...

Then Joshua ordered, "Open up the cave and bring the five kings out to me." So Joshua's men removed the five kings from the cave...and brought them before Joshua.

Joshua summoned all of Israel and ordered his army officers, "Place your feet on the necks of these kings." So they placed their feet upon their necks! Then Joshua said to his officers, "Never be afraid of your enemies or let them discourage you. Be strong and filled with courage! Yahweh is going to do to all your enemies what he's done to these kings!"

Then Joshua had the kings executed and hanged on five trees, and he left them there until evening. At sunset, Joshua ordered them taken down from the trees and thrown into the cave where they had been hiding. He had large stones rolled over the mouth of the cave, and they remain there to this day. (Joshua 10:17–27)

Joshua's men imprisoned five Amorite kings and set as guards over the cave where they were hiding until he had defeated all their armies. Then his men opened the cave and brought out the kings. Joshua instructed his officers to put their feet on the necks of these kings as a symbolic act of their victory. Then Joshua executed the five kings and hanged them on five trees. These five kings can be seen as our five senses, five kings over our natural realm. Without the Holy Spirit and the revelation that he gives us, our five natural senses rule over us and compel us to obey what they tell us. But there is a realm outside of these five "kings" that must dominate our lives—the realm of Spirit life in Christ.

Our human mindset and opinions are like a cave and tomb where the natural realm operates without the Spirit of God. In the same way that Joshua placed guards over the cave of Makkedah, so Jesus (our Joshua) set guardians over the church as spiritual leaders and examples for us. Also, in the same way that Joshua executed the five kings, so Jesus has silenced all the voices accusing and condemning us (see Romans 8:1–6), and Jesus has set us free from our self-life. He crucified us with him (see Galatians

2:20), and our old identities are dead and buried. The Amorite kings were placed on five trees, so our bondage to the natural world and our five senses were likewise placed on the "tree" of Calvary. Our old life is dead and buried. We no longer live submitted to sin's power because Jesus gives us new life and a new identity. These are but a few of the lessons we learn from Joshua 10. What a chapter of miracles!

LET'S PRAY

Lord Jesus, you have accomplished so much for me. Every victory in my life is because of you. You once made the sun stand still for Joshua, so today, I ask you for a great miracle. I ask you…(Now, pray your greatest request before God and believe that he will answer you!) I ask you to do this in Jesus' name and for his sake. Amen.

36

ONE BATTLE AFTER ANOTHER

YAHWEH empowered Joshua to conquer the whole region, including the hill country, the southern desert, the western foothills, and the mountain slopes. He conquered all the kings of the land and left no survivors. Everything that breathed was slaughtered—as YAHWEH, the God of Israel, had commanded. Joshua's conquest stretched from Kadesh Barnea to Gaza, and from Goshen to Gibeon. Joshua conquered all their kings and their lands in a single campaign, for YAHWEH, the God of Israel, fought for his people. Finally, Joshua and all the Israelite army returned to their base camp in Gilgal.

JOSHUA 10:40–43

Every follower of Jesus can expect a life of spiritual battles. Often, it seems like one battle after another. Although we are called to a victorious and glorious life with Christ, we are not called to a life of ease and comfort. We are told to deny ourselves, pick up the cross, and live our lives as good soldiers of Jesus Christ (see 2 Timothy 2:3–4).

The tenth chapter of Joshua is filled with warfare, as Joshua fights one city after another and conquers them all. This chapter lists no less than seven victories in order to establish the Israelites in their land and make the name of Yahweh famous. The enemies fall like dominos with the power of God driving Joshua and his men forward. The enemies of God were nothing before this champion named Joshua.

There is a lesson for us today in this chapter. The Joshua generation must be those who identify and eliminate everything in our lives that hinders our life in God. These "-ites" often are hidden in our heart and must be dealt with. Our weapons are spiritual, and our warfare is not against people but against powers of darkness that limit God's victory within us (see Ephesians 6:10–18). If you want to conquer a city, you must first let Jesus conquer your heart. The utter destruction of the cities of the land was not an easy task for Joshua, and our heavenly Joshua must have our "yes" in order for him to complete his task of taking his "land" within us. We must set apart the "promised land" of our hearts for God alone, with neither compromise nor hidden sin. It is our responsibility to seek out and destroy anything in our lives that might corrupt a single-hearted devotion and pure love for a holy God (see Matthew 5:29–30; 2 Corinthians 11:3). With God's divine grace, nothing is impossible (see Matthew 19:26; Luke 1:37). We will share the likeness of Jesus and become the radiant, look-alike partners of the Son of God (see Revelation 19:7–8).

Did you notice the words "YAHWEH empowered Joshua to conquer the whole region"? There is only one person who can defeat the giants in the land and the giants in your heart. It is our heavenly Joshua who can never be defeated. When he fights alongside us, we are led in one continual triumph. It was not simply one battle after another but rather one victory after another. One single campaign and Joshua devasted the entire land. And one single triumphant procession with Jesus and we, too, will triumph. "Thanks be to God, who always leads us as captives in Christ's triumphal procession and uses us to spread the aroma of the knowledge of him everywhere" (2 Corinthians 2:14 NIV).

THE WARFARE CONTINUES—JOSHUA'S NORTHERN CONQUEST

> When the news of Israel's southern victories reached King Jabin of Hazor, he organized a massive coalition to fight against Israel...King Jobab... the king of Shimron, the king of Achshaph, the kings of the northern hill country, the kings of the Jordan Valley...the kings of the foothills...kings in the heights of Dor, the eastern and western Canaanite kings, the Amorite kings, the Hittite kings, the Perizzite kings, the Jebusite kings...the Hivite kings...They came out in full force with a multitude of horses and chariots. Their vast armies were as numerous as the grains of sand on the seashore. All these kings and their enormous armies joined forces...to fight against Israel. (Joshua 11:1–5)

It was the Lord who gave the victory to Joshua against this massive coalition of kings and armies. Virtually every ethnic group that inhabited the land came against Joshua, which only made God's victory even greater. God gave Joshua a powerful promise, and Joshua took hold of it unwaveringly and obeyed. "Yahweh spoke to Joshua, saying, 'Don't be afraid of them; by this time tomorrow, I, Yahweh, will have them all lying slain before Israel. After the battle, cripple their horses and burn their chariots'" (v. 6).

This promise works for us too. Receive it! Don't be afraid of them. Every single enemy you face is going to be handed over to you. Every single source of depression, defeat, unbelief, and fear will be crushed. God says, *I'm going to reverse it, and your enemies will be defeated!* How? Joshua obeyed the Lord. Listen, dear friend, this is the key to conquering. Where is the victory? It's in the Lord Jesus Christ. He's the one who gives it to us. In your marriage difficulties, in your financial pressures, in your relational issues—obedience to Jesus' specific instruction is the key. God will give you the victory, and you, too, must rise up and obey.

So, Joshua laid hold of God's promise of victory and fully obeyed God's directions even to the point of crippling the enemy's horses. Why cripple the horses? This is significant for three reasons.

1. It meant these demonic powers would never chase them again. They were powerless, literally and figuratively "hamstrung."

2. Furthermore, the horses and chariots had to be eliminated because God didn't want his people to put their trust in horses and chariots. He wanted them so weak and dependent upon the God of power that

no matter what enemy they faced, they would always remember that God was big enough to conquer. They didn't need horses, and they didn't need chariots. They needed faith and confidence in God.

3. He wanted the horses disabled so the Canaanites could not use them again as part of their demonic worship, as was their custom. So, God covered all the bases, making it clear that the victory was his for his people and his over their enemies.

Even though this epic battle takes up only a few verses in Joshua 11, it actually lasted many years: "Joshua waged war with all those kings over a long period" (v. 18).[22] That "long period" ended up being a seven-year period of bloody warfare against very fierce kingdoms, some of which were the giants of the land, the Anakites, "a race of giants" (vv. 21–22). These were a people who stood about nine to eleven feet tall. Now, it just so happened that one of their descendants was a giant named Goliath, who would later face David and God's people in battle. Joshua was given the commission and charged by God to go against every giant and conquer them.

This was an incredible military victory, and it is time for some incredible spiritual victories for the Joshua generation, victories so incredible that you won't have anybody to thank but God alone. You won't glorify any man, any mighty prophet, or any super-spiritual event. I want incredible victories, don't you? I want victories that have no solution except the divine intervention from heaven.

LET'S PRAY

God of Glory, please forgive me for every time I have limited you. I see now that your power has no limit in spite of the great forces that have come against me and my family. I bow before your greatness. Give me supernatural grace to rise and not fall, to walk and not stumble, to fight and not give up. I owe it all to you, my King and my God. Amen.

37

POSSESSING THE INHERITANCE

*Many years passed, and Joshua was a very old man. One day,
YAHWEH spoke to him: "Although you have reached a ripe old age,
a great deal of land remains for you to conquer."*

JOSHUA 13:1

The first twelve chapters of Joshua are about conquering the land, and the last twelve chapters are about possessing the land. In this way, Joshua is a two-part story and gives us this powerful lesson: it isn't over when we receive the promises because we are also called to *possess the promises*. We can be given every good thing God wants us to have and win every spiritual battle, but if we don't stand on it, possess it, and walk in it, then our spirituality is but a fantasy. God wants us to not only win the battles, but he wants us also to "take the land" and take possession of all he's given us.

God was saying, "Joshua, there's more. There is more for you. Don't settle yet." At this time Joshua was likely one hundred years old. At this "ripe old age," God was telling Joshua that there were very large areas of land he still needed to possess. We must apply this to our own hearts. It doesn't matter how long you've been a Christian, how many anointed wells you've drawn from, how many people have laid hands on you, how many conferences and revival centers you've visited, or how many moves of God you've been a part of. There are still very large areas of inheritance left to obtain. There is a large territory yet waiting for you to discover and occupy.

IT IS ALL YOURS...SO TAKE IT

Spiritually, there is more "land" for you to possess, and our promised land is the fullness of Christ. Friend, Jesus is our inheritance. He is the One we are after. We are pursuing him, not some self-focused spirituality. Why would we want to be "spiritual" without Christ? Why would we want to be a "somebody" in the church without the fullness of the life of Christ? Why would anybody want to have a ministry without the power and vibrant glory of the life of Jesus? His life in us is full, complete, satisfying, and enjoyable, but there are still very large areas of that higher life that we have yet to touch. There are vast, panoramic vistas just waiting for the church of Jesus Christ to explore and enjoy.

There must be a reality of Jesus Christ that we can enter in which we taste and see and discover that the Lord is good. I want to touch more of the life of Christ, don't you? I want to experience all the promises. That was the message God gave to Joshua and the message he is speaking to the Joshua generation. Now listen to the instructions God gave to Joshua:

> You still must conquer the land of the Sidonians…
> As the people of Israel advance, I myself will drive
> out these peoples from before you! Divide the
> land among the tribes of Israel exactly as I have
> commanded you. (v. 6)

Here, God gives Joshua his next task. Joshua had already conquered the enemy. He was basically in control of the land, but now God wanted Joshua to divide the land into portions and give it away. Listen, Joshua conquered for the benefit of somebody else. You see, what made Joshua a great man was that he caused others to inherit their portion. God is looking for men and women of the Spirit today who aren't merely going after something for themselves, but instead they want to cause *others* to go into *their* inheritance.

THINK GENERATIONALLY BECAUSE GOD DOES!

We, Brian and Candice, are grandparents and great-grandparents. And although we've had tremendous experiences in Christ on the mission field and in ministry here in North America, we have a passion yet burning in our hearts to leave behind something for this next generation. We all should eagerly desire to leave behind for this emerging Joshua generation a legacy of love, wisdom, riches, and blessing. We want to lay up a spiritual inheritance for those who follow us. Decades after our funerals, we want the people of God to go way beyond anything that we may have attained or even dreamed of attaining. You see, there is so much yet to possess. What distinguishes Joshua as a godly leader and a great man of notable character was that he did what he did…*for others.*

It will be a test for you in your life. Count on it. Sooner or later, you will face the test of whether you can let go and build for somebody else. Everything the great apostle Paul built and established he later turned over to other people. You see, ultimately, our ministry and calling is a calling of abandonment to Christ. We leave our present life in his hands, and we leave our future life in his hands. We leave the works of today in his capable care and trust that he will use it all to build a wonderful tomorrow. We have a duty to lay treasures up for a generation yet to come. So let me ask you: What are you building, and whom are you going to build it for? Let the ultimate purpose of all you accomplish be for others to go in and possess *their* inheritance. This is true joy and true success in ministry.

> The benevolent man leaves an inheritance that
> endures to his children's children,
> but the wealth of the wicked is treasured up for
> the righteous. (Proverbs 13:22)

INHERITING THE LAND

The word *inheritance* is a theme of the last twelve chapters of Joshua. It occurs well over fifty times. The people *inherited* the land, and when you inherit something, that means you didn't earn it. You didn't work for it. You didn't win it. They inherited the promises, and so do we. It was God's land to give, and he gave it freely to his children. An inheritance just comes without you doing anything except being in the right place at the right time. The land was owned by God. The people simply leased the land from him. Think about that! The Lord is your landlord. And your "rent" is obedience to the will of God and the Word of God.

On Mount Sinai, when God thundered out his promises, the people answered, "We will everything the LORD has said" (Exodus 19:8 NIV). They made a covenant and a commitment that they would follow the ways of the Lord. Deuteronomy 28 shows us the blessings of God that come upon the willing and obedient. You see, the "rent" they paid to possess God's land was obedience to him. They couldn't win it or possess it without that yielded heart. Jesus fulfilled all the righteous requirements of the law on our behalf, and now by faith in him, we also possess the promises with a yielded and obedient heart. Praise God!

LET'S PRAY

Father God, you are my joy and my delight! Knowing you is to know life eternal. My treasure, my wealth is my relationship with you. Take my life and direct me throughout this day. Everything in me cries out to you. I want to know you more. I want to love you more. I want to follow your ways and not my own. Make it happen, Lord God. Amen.

38

LESSONS ABOUT YOUR INHERITANCE

"Little by little I will drive them out before you, until you increased enough to take possession of the land."

EXODUS 23:30 NIV

Let me give you six lessons in the following chapters about this inheritance that we have in Jesus Christ. We will spend the most time on the first one because I believe it's the most important for us to understand.

LESSON 1

This is the first lesson we must learn: *your inheritance is received little by little.* In his wisdom, God didn't give *all* the land to *all* the people *all* at once. We want everything right now, but that's not how

God allots the inheritance. That's not how God distributes the destiny he has for your life. Your inheritance is the fullness of Christ. Although we have his fullness now, it is imparted *little by little.*

All the tribes of Israel did not receive an equal allotment of land. Not every one of the twelve tribes got the same portion. Like it or not—believe it or not—God does not always treat his people equally. That may rock your world a bit, but it is true. You see, those who are not hungry or desperate for more will get a smaller portion, and those who are spiritually passionate and aggressive receive more. Let this be your wake-up call. Not everybody in God's kingdom is equal, and I think we, in our democratic culture, have a difficult time with this reality. It can be hard for some to process the fact that in God's family and God's kingdom, he gives us an inheritance that is commensurate to who we are. For your hunger determines what you receive.

We see this in Jesus' Sermon on the Hillside. He said, "Blessed are the meek, for they will inherit the earth" (Matthew 5:5 NIV). Those who have a spirit of humility and are yielded to the will of God will receive a larger portion. On the other hand, the know-it-alls, the arrogant, the prideful who exaggerate their spirituality, convinced that they are more important than others, are not going to get a big portion because they're not ready to steward it. God wants each one of his children to know that there is an allotment of inheritance, a spiritual possession that he wants us to have, but we're going to have to be humble, desperate, and spiritually passionate enough to go after it.

Each Tribe a Different Portion

The tribes were all unique, and God uniquely dealt with each one of them. This shocks a lot of people when they read Joshua

13–21. God didn't give them all the same, equal part of the land because he is not a "cookie-cutter" kind of God. He has a custom, individualized plan for each of us, and we see this in the church. Some people have a high level of anointing, and others are content with low-level spirituality. God wants to grip us with this reality: we have as much of God as we want. We can have as much of our inheritance as we are ready to possess. This is a principle that has the power to guide you for the rest of your life—and it should! You have the portion of God—right now—that you are content to have. If you are not content to have what you've got, then get going and get some more because it's there for you!

There are yet very great areas of land in Christ that you can possess. That is what God spoke to Joshua, and he is speaking the same counsel to you and me. In his wisdom, God knows what he's doing. He has determined that his children will possess according to our humility and our hunger. Who we are and where we are in our spirituality determine the inheritance we will walk in. Are we thirty-fold? Are we sixty-fold? Are we a hundred-fold? (see Mark 4:20).

Some people settle down and are content with small parcels of God, settling for so little of the feast God has prepared for us. So, beloved, there is more! There is so much more to feed on in the Scriptures. There's so much more Spirit power he wants to baptize you with. He wants you to be conformed to the image of Jesus. He wants you to be naturally supernatural. He wants you to go into the holy realm of the spirit life. There are more realms you can access and more revelation to receive. I want more, don't you? Here's what the Lord once revealed to me: *nothing from your first birth should ever hinder you from claiming what you have been given in your second birth.*

Let me say it clearly: God has given us every spiritual blessing (see Ephesians 1:3). Now, we must possess it and dwell in the fullness of his blessing. Again, we have as much of God as we truly want. The ball is in our court; we decide how much we will receive and the measure of our inheritance. In the next chapter, we'll look at more lessons on obtaining our fullness.

Let's Pray

Lord Jesus, you died so that I would have eternal life and experience its fullness throughout my days. I want more of you. I long for you. I thirst for more of your living water. Satisfy my heart as I seek you throughout this day. I know you will answer my heart's cry for more of your glory. I receive it now! Amen.

39

No Land for the Levites

Moses gave no inheritance of land to the tribe of Levi, but said to them, "Yahweh, the God of Israel, is to be your inheritance."

JOSHUA 13:33

Lesson 2

Lesson number two about our inheritance: *it is a spiritual, heavenly inheritance.* The Levites were priests, and God alone was to be their portion. No land was given to the Levites. The priestly tribe of Levi's descendants were to live from the offerings of the people, not the labor of the land. Later, they were given cities in which they could dwell and pastures in which to raise their livestock, but the Levites themselves were to own no land. Their portion was God himself. And so, we are priests of the living God, and our true inheritance is in heaven, where Christ is seated at the right hand of God. Our gaze must be heavenward (see Colossians 3:1–4; 1 Peter 2:4–8; Revelation 1:6).

This distinction made by God bears significance when we study the unique, New Testament account of Ananias and Sapphira in Acts 5:1–11. They were killed because they lied about a portion of land they had sold. Do you know what caused them to commit this sin? It was jealousy. You see, they had witnessed a Levite, a man named Joseph, sell his piece of land. They all knew that Levites weren't supposed to own land in Israel. But something powerful was happening—revival was breaking out! Revival came to the heart of this man, Joseph, and he repented. He made things right, sold the land (which he was not supposed to own), and took the profit from the sale and gave it as an offering. He brought it in holy dedication to the Lord, which was what he ought to have done.

Sadly, instead of inspiring Ananias and Sapphira to greater devotion, Joseph's actions moved them to competition. They ended up doing the same thing with their own land, but this deceptive couple deviously kept back a portion of the profit while claiming that they had given it entirely over to God. Here is the point: God will choose our spiritual inheritance for us. Whatever inheritance you have, God is the one who has allotted it to you. His ways are *always* best, and once we possess our allotted portion, we can be content with what God has given us in Christ. We never need to compete or be jealous of someone else's inheritance.

Lesson 3

Lesson number three is this: *be encouraged in your journey.* You have already received your inheritance in Christ. You aren't waiting for it. In the natural world, somebody has to die before you get your inheritance, but in the spiritual realm, you, too, must die to this world before you get your inheritance. This is a death to self, vanity, pride that says you deserve it, and self-righteousness that says you have earned it. No, it is an *inheritance.* God gave it to you because of his love, his kindness, and his mercy and because he knows what you're able to steward in Christ. As you continue in maturity and love, you will be able to steward more and more of it.

Lesson 4

Lesson four is this: *we're never too old to make new conquests of faith.* If you ever feel like you have passed your prime in God, just think of Caleb. Caleb was eighty-five years old when he asked for his mountain. Here's what Caleb said:

> I was forty years old when Moses, Yahweh's servant, sent me from Kadesh Barnea to spy out the land of Canaan, and I brought back an honest and accurate report. I have been faithful and obedient to Yahweh, my God. But my fellow spies who went with me only discouraged the people and made their hearts shrink back with fear. On that day, Moses made an oath and promised me, "Every part of the land your feet tread upon shall be an inheritance for you and your descendants forever because you were loyal to Yahweh, my God." (Joshua 14:7–9)

God gave to Caleb virtually the same promise he gave to Joshua: wherever you walk on the land, that's going to be your portion. So, Caleb waited…faithfully, and now his time had finally come, not a moment late.

> So here I am. It's been forty-five years since
> Yahweh made this promise to Moses, when Israel
> journeyed through the wilderness. Yahweh has
> preserved me, an eighty-five-year-old man, to this
> day. (v. 10)

At eighty-five, Caleb is determined to have all God promised. Listen, friend, God keeps his promises. If there are some things you have been waiting for, be like Caleb and don't give up. Hold on! Your promises will not pass their expiration date. God remembers, and he is working on getting your inheritance into your hands even now. Let faith arise within your heart. You, too, will walk in your promised land. Caleb goes on to say this:

> Now give me the hill country that Yahweh prom-
> ised me on that day. You yourself were there and
> heard the report that the Anakim lived there in
> strong and fortified cities. I know that with the
> power of Yahweh helping me, I will drive them
> out, just as Yahweh said! (v. 12)

Give me…what Yahweh *promised me.* At eighty-five, Caleb still wanted mountains. He wasn't thinking of retirement on a nice golf course somewhere; he wanted his rugged hill country. Don't ever think that you're too old, you've done too much wrong, or you've been disqualified by a speckled past. God knew just what he was getting into when he chose you, and he still chose you. God wants to give you a passion right now in your journey to press on and walk upon your own high places, your own mountains. Caleb was an overcomer because he had faith to press on. Let's grab hold of his life message and press on as well until we have all God has destined for us.

Let's Pray

Wonderful Father, I am so thankful to know you and to serve you. I want to leave every trace of passivity behind. I want to passionately pursue you with all my heart. Enflame my soul, enlarge my capacity to know you. I want to know you not as a distant Father, but I want to know you as friend, companion, and shepherd. Open my heart to greater fullness. Amen.

40

WALKING IN MY FULL INHERITANCE

"If imperfect parents know how to lovingly take care of their children and give them what they need, how much more will the perfect heavenly Father give the Holy Spirit's fullness when his children ask him."

LUKE 11:13

Let's finish this forty-day walk through our promised land with these final two lessons.

LESSON 5

Lesson five is this: *God wants all his people to walk in their full inheritance.* There is no question that it is in God's heart to give us good things. The question is *how much do you want?* What are *you* asking for? Caleb asked for a mountain and got it. His daughter, Aksah, asked for a field and springs of water. She got it (see Joshua 15:17–19). Maybe you have never been baptized in the Holy Spirit. Perhaps you have never entered prophetic revelation. Maybe you don't think your dreams are important, and so you haven't even pursued them. Perhaps you don't understand the supernatural realm and have yet to touch and enter the glory realm of God.

Why don't you ask him today? Why don't you start right now and simply ask? Ask for more! He wants to give you more; that is who he is. If you don't have a specific request, then ask for the specifics. If you don't have any passion to ask, then ask for passion to ask! Ask him for the desire to want more than what you have. Just begin to ask. Begin to cry out. God will hear your voice just like he heard Caleb's voice. He is not a respecter of persons. Your cry will pierce his ears and his heart, ascending into the courts of heaven every bit as much as Moses' cry or Joshua's cry or Elijah's cry. Your cry before God can be heard, so it is time to ask. Beloved, God will give you your heart's desire. What are you asking for? God will not withhold your inheritance. Don't sit back and watch other people press in and touch the hem of his garment while you remain unwell. You must be the one who rises up and says, "This is the day. This is the hour. I will take what God has promised to me."

You will not be looked over by God. Friend, your heavenly Dad has his loving gaze fixed on you. No matter your past, present, or future. No matter your age, gender, or ethnicity. No matter your intellect or education. All of God's children have a claim to their inheritance.

Perhaps you have never considered this, but Ephraim and Manasseh were not from the original twelve tribes of Israel. They were actually Israel's *grandchildren*. Symbolically, this shows us God wants everybody, even the young, to take their inheritance. And God also made sure that the women received their inheritance. You see, the daughters of God have an inheritance. God's culture is that women get what they've been destined to have. Kingdom reality is the culture of God. We must take hold of the Scriptures and make them our culture. What God says is what's true and right. Whether we're a minority, disadvantaged, female, an outcast of society, or forgotten by the church—it's irrelevant in this great kingdom enterprise. We take what's ours because God has given it. He wants all of us, no matter what, to take our inheritance.

LESSON 6

Finally, lesson six is this: *no one can complain.* God is the one who assigns the place where we live, the gifts we have, the impact of our lives on others, and the blessings and rewards that we receive. God is the One. If you're in a place in your life with which you're unhappy, don't blame God. You must deal with that and work it out with heaven but realize that God is good, and the portion he has given you is also good.

You see, that's the identity God wants you to have. He wants to give you the security of knowing that he is in charge; he really is. People can't ruin you irreparably. The devil can't keep your goods. People can't close doors that God opens for you. God is the one who is ruling this universe. I want to interrupt your depression with a word from your sponsor: God is in charge of the whole wide world. He has assigned you a portion, and it is *good*. He has given you a cup, and it's pleasing. He has made your lot secure, and you can rest confidently in him. Our portion is our inheritance, and our cup is our enjoyment of that inheritance. God gives us our portion, and then he gives us a cup from which we drink of that portion. Our inheritance is a portion *in the land of Christlikeness*—the fulfillment of the satisfying Christ-life within us—but he also assigns us the cup from which we drink and participate in that life.

God is so good. The mercy of the Lord is so real. He is our chosen portion, and he fully satisfies. When we understand that God is the one who has given us all things, we will rejoice with a grateful heart. An unthankful heart opens the door for the enemy to come in and steal what the Lord has already apportioned for us. Thankfulness safeguards our enjoyment of his goodness.

God will give us grace to enjoy our portion, our destiny. We don't need to worry about whether we're going to get to our destiny. We also don't need to worry about missing it—taking the wrong job, marrying the wrong person, moving to the wrong town. We don't need to worry at all! Worry reveals that we think we are bigger than God, wiser than God, and more capable than God. Worry looks like this: panic, fear, anxiety, and the cares of this life that choke the word of the kingdom from coming forth in us. When those things fill our heart, the life of Christ is stifled, and we cannot enter the destiny of a "delightful inheritance" God has for us. Our delightful inheritance is knowing Jesus Christ. We can know him! Whether you're in a pit or a palace, you can know Christ. The lie of the devil is that you can only know Christ when things are good. It's a lie of Satan that you can only enter the enjoyment of Christ when there's no pain in your life. Well, I hate to break this to you, but that probably will never happen. We will have pain, hardships, toils, and labors, no matter how great our faith.

Jesus Christ is our delightful, promised land. He is so pleasant and fully satisfying. Beloved, I commend to you the enjoyment of Christ. I say to the Joshua generation: don't wait to possess your inheritance. Press in and enjoy the Lord right now. Follow the passionate pursuit of knowing him—his heart, his voice, and his ways. Don't passively wait for fair-weather conditions in life; instead, make your moment and take your moment. Ask for your mountain, and then enjoy every part and parcel of it. You have a bright future, and his name is Jesus, so run into his arms and possess every promise.

LET'S PRAY

Father, I ask you to sweep over me with a fresh new passion for walking into my full inheritance and for taking the good portion that I have in Christ. Like Caleb, I ask you to give me my mountain. Like Joshua, today, I receive your Word that there are yet very large areas of land for me to possess. There is more, and I want it all. Lord, I choose to be like Othniel and Aksah, who were bold and asked for what they wanted. I declare before you today that I will not live without the enjoyment of Christ. Take away everything that would keep me from enjoying my delightful inheritance. Lord, I choose to taste and see your goodness in the land of the living and feast at your table of sweetest communion. Help me not to shrink back or lose heart so that I will walk in all the promises you have given to me. Thank you, Father, in Jesus' name. Amen.

Joshua Defeats Thirty-One Kings

Joshua captured all their kings and executed them. Joshua waged war with all those kings over a long period...By the power of Yahweh, Joshua conquered them all.

Joshua 11:17-19

Sweet victory! Yahweh's commander, Joshua, conquered thirty-one kings. The sun stood still for God's mighty warrior. Hailstones fell from the sky. Victory after victory. No one could stand before Joshua, just as God had promised him (see Joshua 1:5). In Joshua 12:9-24, we have a list of thirty-one kings whom Joshua conquered in his promised land. Is there a hidden message in this list of defeated kings? We're going to look at the symbolic strongholds and what they represent in each of our lives and have a dismantling party.

So, who were these kings that Joshua (Jesus) defeated? Do their names have any significance for us today? I believe they do. You see, every city in the promised land had a king. These kings are pictures of the principalities and powers, the dark forces that are in this world. The meaning of the names of the principalities of these thirty-one kings could represent the thirty-one strongholds[23] that dull our understanding of the finished work of Christ for us. These thirty-one strongholds or "kings" love to rear their ugly heads in the church and in our lives if we allow it. They often manifest as competition, strife, and jealousy that tend to divide and conquer the body of Christ worldwide. These are powers that resist our entrance into the heavenlies. They dull the revelation of the finished work of Christ, and they try to lure us back to old Adam-life that has already been defeated in Christ and endeavors to hold us back from our promises in God. Let's take a deeper look at each one and discuss how they can be toppled.

Jesus Defeats Our Darkness

King #1 is the king of Jericho, a walled city that was dedicated to demonic powers. *Jericho* means "city of the moon." This walled city represents impossible obstacles and occultic power. This is the first king (stronghold) that must come down. Your darkness must be defeated! You see, there is no impossible obstacle with God. When things seem impossible, we're actually fighting and struggling with an illusion. The reality is not your obstacle. The reality is the God who knocks down obstacles. When God is finally viewed as bigger than your walled city, victory is near, and demonic kings are about to bow down. Israel's destiny was to defeat every "king," every dark power that opposed the light of God. This is your destiny as well; you break through every wall and limitation, for you are a light bearer in this world.

THE SPIRIT OF THIS WORLD IS DEFEATED

King #2 is the king of Ai. *Ai* is the Hebrew word for "a heap of ruins." The world without God is nothing more than a heap of ruins. Ai is the spirit of this world, the corruption of this world, and the corrupt alliances within the world system. That is a king that must be uprooted and destroyed in the body of Christ (see 1 John 2:17). We have a choice to turn our face and focus away from Ai (the world) and toward Bethel (God's house), for Ai is "near Bethel." Wherever we put our focus will govern our lives. We must consciously choose well and put God ever before us and always first. Your choice is between a heap of ruins and the house of God.

COUNTERFEIT SPIRITUALITY

King #3 is the king of Jerusalem. In Joshua's day, a counterfeit, wicked king ruled over Jerusalem. Many centuries later, King David would rule over this redeemed city. But the Jerusalem of Joshua's day speaks of counterfeit apostleship, counterfeit leadership, and counterfeit spirituality that need to be broken in our lives. Some Christians have misplaced and misguided loyalties to corrupt systems. Any corrupt system, whether in the world or in the church, must be abandoned, and the body of Christ must place their loyalties in the kingdom of God (see Matthew 6:33), and then the anointing and blessing of God will flow unhindered. But if you're seeking to be "somebody" in a church, seeking to rub elbows with those you consider to be the most important spiritual leaders, and making that the basis of your identity, then you have misguided loyalty. Conquering the king of Jerusalem means toppling a false identity to a counterfeit kingdom.

Restoration of Fellowship

King #4 is the king of Hebron, whose name was Hoham. *Hebron* means "fellowship" or "union," and *Hoham* means "he crushed." This is the mindset that represents a lack of communion with God. This king wants to get between us and our relationship with the Father. His goal is to crush you and break this fellowship (your enjoyment of God). That which can hinder our intimacy with God can be material possessions, unhealthy relationships, hobbies, sinful habits, and so on. Every sin and even things that weigh or slow us down from our relationship with God must be cast off (see Hebrews 12:1–2). Anything that hinders fellowship with God must be removed from our hearts. If we don't deal with it ourselves, we can count on God to deal with it. He is always busy removing things that hinder love. He's a jealous God!

Pride and Rebellion

King #5 that our heavenly Joshua will defeat is the king of Jarmuth. *Jarmuth* means a "high place" or "lifted up," and it speaks of pride. The name of the king of Jarmuth was Piram, and his name means "wild donkey." Doesn't that sound like the pride and untamed rebellion of our culture, where everybody pushes to have their way no matter what the cost to others? This stronghold will cause us to leave in our wake a swath of wounded people and broken relationships. This demonic mindset must be overthrown. Only Jesus can conquer this fifth stronghold of the human heart.

SELF-RELIANCE

Let's look at king #6, the king of Lachish, which represents an unteachable heart, for *Lachish* means "impregnable." It is an ungodly self-reliance that trusts in our own cleverness. Lachish is a picture of that strong, arrogant, elitist pride that rises up and says, "I have what it takes to finish what God started. I have what it takes in my own nature, strength, and cleverness to make it all happen." It's very easy for some Christians to fall into the trap of thinking that God needs the strength of *their* personality to accomplish *his* work, but the exact opposite is true. God is going to overcome our human strength and strong personality just like he broke the hip and the inner being of Jacob, who limped his way into the promised land (see Genesis 32:25, 31). Many of us will also limp into our inheritance because God is magnified and exalted through our weaknesses, not our strengths. May we remember where our help and strength come from.

STUBBORNNESS

King #7 is the king of Eglon. *Eglon* means "bull-like," and he represents the aggressive, arrogant, and intimidating ways that convince us that we are always in the right. But truly wise and humble people are those who have been taught the ways of Christ, who is gentle and tenderhearted (see Matthew 11:29). These are the ones who will win others, not wound others. We are to be "lamb-like," not "bull-like." Those who wrestle with this king will discover that only King Jesus can conquer him.

SHARP, BITTER WORDS

King #8, the king of Gezer, is a king we must all deal with. *Gezer* means "steep," "sharp," or "to cut." This is the king who boasts of his sharpness of tongue. Have you ever heard someone who communicates with a biting, harsh, and critical speech? Let me tell you, that is such a stronghold with some people, and the bitterness of their words ruin their fruit for God (see James [Jacob] 3:10). The Lord must have control of our tongues so that he can use us to spread his sweetness wherever we go.

POLITICAL SPIRIT

King #9 has been a temptation to believers from the beginning of the church. *Debir* means "speaker" or "orator," and the king of Debir loves to pontificate and persuade. He represents a political spirit that seeks to infiltrate the church, but God's kingdom does not operate by political opinion or political powers. It does not bow to majority rule. God's kingdom has a King, and his name is Jesus. He is the one who governs the universe—eternally. He is not going to be toppled from his throne. His edict is sovereign; he speaks, and it shall be done, end of discussion. Since Jesus' throne will never fall, this political spirit that infiltrates the body of Christ to form alliances between the church and politics will only bring competition and strife. May this king fall!

DEFENSIVENESS

The king of Geder is king #10. *Geder* is the Hebrew word for "a wall," and it represents that wall of defensiveness that rises in our hearts when we are opposed or rejected. It's the default defense mechanism we resort to when we feel exposed or uncovered. When selfish motives and soulish actions are confronted, that wall suddenly goes up and says, "Stop right there." Human nature just doesn't want to be confronted and exposed by revelation truth, and when we are, we often feel threatened, and the wall of defense comes up. Receiving truth, even hard truth, is necessary for spiritual growth and development.

DEPRESSION

King #11 is of Hormah. The word *Hormah* speaks of defeat and depression, for it means "devastated," "ruined," or "banned." There are some of us still living in that little town of "Hormahville," discouraged and depressed. When we become comfortable with defeat, we begin to make it our pet and continue to coddle our self-pity instead of viewing it as the worst vile serpent that ever latched onto us in our life. With depression as your friend, you can't rise and possess your promises. Why not serve it an eviction notice and watch it be defeated. Drive out King Hormah, for Jesus' sake. Your "Joshua" can defeat this king (see Deuteronomy 31:8).

LAWLESSNESS

King #12 rules Arad. The Hebrew word *Arad* means "wild fugitive" or "one who refuses to submit [to the law or Word of God]." This king represents lawlessness. That lawlessness in the body of Christ—that sense of being above principles, above character, above integrity, and above the Word—is a vile king within the church that must be toppled. The lawless must have no place in the kingdom of God (see Matthew 7:23).

SELF-RIGHTEOUSNESS

The king of Libnah is king #13. *Libnah* means "white" or "whitewashed" and represents hypocrisy and self-righteousness, which appears calm, cool, and collected in the church, but it's vile. If you give it enough time, the stench of sinful flesh will come through the painted facade (see Matthew 23:27). The moral decay of one's heart will be revealed because hidden things will always be exposed by God in time.

Perverted Justice

King #14 is the king of Adullam, which speaks of the rule of men, the insistence on having our rights, even though our only right is to believe in Jesus (see John 1:12). *Adullam* means "justice [rights] of the people." This is an influence that often rules in the church, and it has access through hearts unsubmitted to God. *Adullam* can also be translated as "a sealed-off place." That is a good description of a proud heart, sealed off from the truth of our need in Christ. We are destined to walk in victory, so we must push aside this proud king and let Jesus reign supreme. Every shade of perverted justice and demanding our own rights must be laid at the feet of Jesus, our Joshua.

Control Spirit (False Authority)

The king of Makkedah is king #15. *Makkedah* means "the place of shepherds" or "to drive (lead) by force." It represents false leadership and the "shepherding" spirit of false spiritual authority. Every authority has a delegated realm, and when we go outside of that realm, we stretch ourselves into what should belong only to God. This king is a false authority that usurps the Holy Spirit. We must not walk in a control spirit or give place to it. We must never give a person the place in our hearts meant to be governed by God alone (see Exodus 20:3).

Religious Spirit

The king of Bethel is king #16, a king that our Joshua must defeat. *Bethel* means "the house of God," and it represents the religious spirit. A religious spirit soothes the unconverted soul and convinces the vile that they are okay in their sin. It will work to convince people that if you simply go to church, get baptized, and drop an occasional offering to God, then he will be happy enough with you. Overthrow the religious spirit in your life that wants you to be content with form and ritual instead of fire and relationship. Our spirituality is a grace-gift, not a duty nor a work of the flesh. Don't settle for the counterfeit when God wants to give you true intimacy.

DRUNKENNESS (LOVE OF PLEASURE)

Sadly, the king of Tappuah, king #17, has taken some believers hostage. *Tappuah* is the Hebrew word for "apple" or "distillation" or, in essence, "drunkenness." It is a demonic power that incites drunkenness in the body of Christ. We are called to be vigilant warriors, but this king wants us in a spiritual stupor, so drunk on indulgence in alcohol or other worldly pleasures that our spiritual senses are dull, and we, therefore, are rendered powerless and ineffective for the kingdom of heaven (see Proverbs 21:17).

SHAME (SELF-CONDEMNATION)

King #18 is the mighty king of Hepher, who has conquered many. *Hepher* means "a pit." This is the spirit of shame and condemnation that comes through a horrible failure in life. Condemnation and a pit-dwelling mentality will tell us to just give up in hopelessness. For some reason, we adopt perfectionism and believe the lie that we have to be absolutely perfect before God will love us, but that is the furthest thing from the truth. Actually, right here and right now, you are perfect in the Lord Jesus Christ. His love settled down upon you even before you were born because he chose you in him and made you holy before the foundations of the world. So, there is no reason for shame. Can you imagine a shame-free month? Can you imagine for the next 365 days living outside of that pit of condemnation and never going back, never entering the realm of shame ever again? Free and shameless living is your portion when our Joshua overthrows King Hepher.

SELF-SUFFICIENCY

King #19, the king of Aphek, speaks of self-sufficiency. *Aphek* is the Hebrew word for "strength" and is the root word from which we get "fortress." This stronghold sounds like, "I don't need anybody. I don't need any help. Don't help me. I can handle it." But God didn't make us to "handle it" all alone. He made us to need people and to need him. That self-sufficient mentality is a vice, a form of pride, and a sin that has set itself up as a king in the hearts of many. Let your heavenly Joshua come topple Aphek so you can learn a new way of interdependence and healthy community within the family of God (see Romans 12:5).

COMPLACENCY

Many today have no upward vision or passion to move forward because of king #20, the king of Lasharon. *Lasharon* means "like a plain" and represents passivity, complacency, barrenness, and low-level, earthbound living. When this king rules, our eyesight is stuck on this world instead of the heavenly realm. It produces a life of hopelessness. Many of us have experienced so much disappointment that it has affected our willingness to dream with God. We don't want to get our hopes up because we fear being let down again. No matter what has happened in the past, God has good plans for our future (see Jeremiah 29:11). It is time to hope again!

STRIFE

King #21 is Jabab of Madon. *Jobab* means "desert" and "pain and crying," and *Madon* means "strife," "argumentative," or "divisive." This is the mindset of wanting to debate, argue, and prove yourself right. It is rooted in self-defense and projecting self-righteousness. The king of Madon leads to the pain and misery of loneliness. It is a *spiritual* loneliness, a sense of being alone in life. Now, you don't have to be a single person to experience that pain. This king pushes people into the "desert" of self-pity and demonic loneliness. God's people are never meant for that, and he will lead us out of that desert into the oasis of intimacy and community if we let him.

STRENGTH OF HUMAN INTELLIGENCE

The name of king #22 is Jabin, king of Hazor. *Jabin* means "intelligence," and *Hazor* means "fortification." Together, Hazor and its king represent the strength of human intelligence. Human intellect can get in the way of the Holy Spirit. There are revelations from God that transcend human knowledge. This spirit of academia tends to project as someone having all the answers. However, this human wisdom is an illusion. Man's wisdom will always fall short in a day of trouble. Even with all our technology, all the vast computers and artificial intelligence of our day, we still can't cure the common cold, much less heal the pains of the human condition. Man's wisdom and knowledge will ultimately fail, but God's wisdom never will. He is the answer to every question (see 1 Corinthians 1:25).

TRADITION

Shimron Meron, king #23, means "the guardian of arrogance." This is the pharisaical spirit that will guard the human traditions rather than the Word of God. There are Christians bound to religious traditions, and they will ignore the Word of God in favor of those traditions (Matthew 23:13). In their loyalty to "the way it's always been" or "the way we've always done it," they miss the freedom available to them and remain in the same old dysfunctions of their lives and those of previous generations. God wants to get us out of any dead, tradition-bound living and move us into the revelation light of the Scriptures, where we can worship him in spirit and truth.

WITCHCRAFT

Of Achshaph, king #24 represents the spirit of witchcraft. *Achshaph* is the Hebrew word for "enchantment." It represents occultic power operating in the church, and if you don't think that a level of demonic activity operates in churches, here is your notice: it can and does, often looking like control, manipulation, or the "strange fire" of man-centered worship. God wants to see that king toppled and King Jesus highly exalted (see Galatians 5:19–21).

DOUBLE-MINDEDNESS

King #25, the king of Taanach, rules over many. *Taanach* means "hard to pass," "sandy," or "the sand on a seashore," and it speaks of soulish whims or double-mindedness. It's the inability to be resolute of will and instead being wishy-washy, flimsy, and weak-willed. Soulish ways are like quicksand, ever taking us downward away from the glory of God. This inability to make godly decisions, stand by them, and then walk them out is essentially building your house on the sand. The slightest wind could blow you into confusion. Everything is relative, and nothing is black and white when this king reigns, so throw him down and build your life on the Rock (see James [Jacob] 1:6–8).

Distraction and an Inability to Focus

Many have been affected by king #26, the king of Megiddo. *Megiddo* means "place of troops" or "crowded place" and represents distraction or anxiety. To be anxious, disturbed, and distracted is to step into the realm of defeat. God's buoyant Spirit will keep us focused on truth, God's goodness, and the hope he has embedded into our future. Only our Joshua can defeat these many distractions that crowd out the peace of God and our life purpose. The Word of God has the answers we need to see this "king" defeated.

False Appearance of Holiness

King #27 is the king of Kedesh. *Kedesh* is the Hebrew word for "holy," "sacred," or "purity." This king represents a works-based holiness that is established on man's standards, not God's. It is the man-made holiness and the standards of sanctification set by men. It looks holy but only goes skin deep. It's cosmetic, not true in character. The church has too much of this shallowness. God doesn't want skin-deep spirituality and superficiality in his people. What happened to true holiness? Our holiness is the life of Christ infused into our nature (see 1 Corinthians 1:30). Let's be those who long to be holy as he is holy (see 1 Peter 1:16).

People Pleasing

The king of Jokneam, king #28, is alive and active in the church world today. *Jokneam* means "possessed (controlled) by the people" and represents celebrity worship and the people-pleasing attitude that infects leaders and people alike. It is the result of our human need for popularity. Unfortunately, this can be a powerful force in the church. If we don't live for the pleasure of God, we will live for the praise of men, wanting to get next to the "big guys" with the really anointed ministries, to be seen with them, to get on the platform with them, and so on.

John the Baptizer, when he really entered into the height of his ministry, was not very popular, and we know what they did with Jesus Christ, who never sinned and only did what was right. He was crucified outside of the camp in humiliation and rejection. It is to be expected that the closer we get to the Son of God, the less popular we will be with men, the fewer people we will have on our mailing list, the less notability and acclaim we will garner, and the more persecution we will incur in our lives. So don't fall before that king and bow to the craving for popularity (see John 12:43). Bow instead to the only Worthy One and make him famous. We need Holy Spirit–possessed leaders who have the fruits of humility, gentleness, and meekness. We need to be men and women of God who fear God, not people.

Worldly Comfort

King #29 is the king of Dor, which speaks of worldly comfort and the need to abide in the comfort zone. *Dor* is the Hebrew word for "dwelling" or "habitation." This king says, "I can't sacrifice. I need my comforts." The king of Dor is the lie that says, "If it is hard or uncomfortable, then it must not be God." Friend, there is a realm in God where it just no longer matters. Nothing matters but him. Whether you have a lot of stuff or you have nothing, it's all the same. Whether you clean toilets or you're the apostle over the whole region, the pay is the same. There's no difference in the body of Christ. It's only obedience that has value. It's only faithfulness to what God tells us to do that matters. So, we forsake the God of worldly comfort if we're going to enter into the land of promise. It is our privilege to do so (see Matthew 16:24).

REFUSAL TO CHANGE

The king of Gilgal is king #30, who holds many back from their promised inheritance. Meaning "to roll," "to turn," or "a circle," *Gilgal* represents the refusal to change. This king will have us dodging the issues and refusing to face reality. Have you ever tried to talk through a tough issue with somebody, and they talk you in circles until you end up coming right back where you started? There's no change, no "owning up," no repentance. That is the refusal to change. This is a demon king in the hearts of many of us and in the church that wants to keep us paralyzed and stuck where we are. We pray for revival, but revival starts with us. We cry out for reformation, but first God wants to reform our own hearts. This spirit will have us avoiding God's conviction and going around and around and never moving into our birthright as children of God. The king of Gilgal must fall so that revival fire can fall.

LOVING PLEASURE MORE THAN GOD

King #31 is the king of Tirzah. The Hebrew word *Tirzah* means "delight" or "pleasing." This king wants us to love worldly pleasures more than we love God. Paul has warned us about this "king" (see 2 Timothy 3:2–4). It is a worldly thing that the enemy wants to tempt you with by dangling it over your heart saying, *If you only had this, you'd be happy.* But Tirzah is an "illegal" pleasure that is not of God nor his will for your life. It's corrupt. It's perverse. It's not pure. It may not keep you from heaven, but it will keep you from your promises (see Matthew 6:33). Therefore, that worldly pleasure is a king that must fall.

YOU ARE CALLED TO CONQUER, NOT COPE!

All these thirty-one kings represent principalities and powers impeding our entrance into the promised realm of the full revelation of Jesus, his work inside of us, and his purpose for each of our lives. Remember, you are called, like Joshua, to take the battle offensively. Why wait when you can start right now? Aggressively take your kingdom by force by insisting that victory breaks loose in your life. Hold nothing back! Oh Joshua generation, life is too short to be a passive participant. Why would we squander our days in low-level spirituality when we've been destined for the stars and the glory realm?

> Wake up! Open your eyes!
> Beautiful Zion, put on your majestic strength!
> Jerusalem, the sacred city,
> put on your glory garments!
> Never again will the unclean enter your gates!
> Arise and shake off your dust!
> Sit enthroned, Jerusalem!
> Break off your shackles of bondage from
> your neck,
> you captive daughter of Zion! (Isaiah 52:1–2)

Increase is coming, so enlarge your tent
and add extensions to your dwelling.
Hold nothing back! Make the tent ropes longer
and the pegs stronger.
You will increase and spread out in every direction.
Your sons and daughters will conquer nations
and revitalize desolate cities. (Isaiah 54:2–3)

Even though most Christians are convinced that God has to do it all, the victory is actually a result of our cooperation with God. A passive spirit says, "*Qué será, será!* Whatever will be, will be." Not so! God has never called us just to cope but to conquer. Yes, your calling is conquering, not coping. Rise up in the splendor of the Son of God. Rise up in the anointing of the Holy One. You have been made more than a conqueror. You've been purchased by blood. So forcefully advance, oh Joshua generation, and lay hold of every blood-bought victory, in Jesus' name. Amen.

Appendix 2

The Cities of Asylum

Hasn't this been a fascinating journey through the book of Joshua? Joshua courageously led about a million people into their God-given inheritance. He was certainly a breaker and a builder. We can see the might and power of the Lord Jesus pictured in the life of Joshua, and in this very hour, Jesus is calling a generation to boldly march into the inheritance of God and possess every promise. We are that generation!

After Joshua settled into the land, the first stronghold he conquered was Jericho, and he fought not with swords and spears but with faith and obedience. It was a faith march. He walked around the walled city as God commanded, and with the trumpet blast and victorious shout, the walled city was overthrown. It is a picture of faith! Anybody can shout when the walls have already fallen, but only those men and women of faith are going to release a victory shout when their walled city still stands in front of them. Friends, we are in our own faith march in this hour.

One city after another fell until, at last, God's people owned it all, and Joshua began to distribute the land as God directed him. Judah got one portion. Issachar got another portion. Simeon got another portion. Zebulon got another portion, and so on. All the twelve tribes of Israel received their inheritance, but not every tribe got the same amount. As we learned in a previous chapter, God does not treat everybody equally. May this truth jolt us out of any lukewarmness: he treats us according to our passion. Jesus said, "To everyone who has [passion, hunger, desire, and so on], more will be given" (Luke 19:26 NIV). You can have as much of God as you want! Now is the time, Joshua generation, for us to rise up with more passion for Jesus than we have ever known because God wants to give us more.

GOD PROVIDES HOPE FOR THE GUILTY

As we conclude our study of the book of Joshua, let's take a look at the provision that God made for cities of asylum within the promised land. Under God's direction, Joshua set up six cities as Moses had instructed in Numbers 35 and Deuteronomy 19. Now, let's look at this account from Joshua 20:

> YAHWEH instructed Joshua: "A person who acci-
> dentally and unintentionally kills someone will
> need a place of asylum—a city where he can run
> for safety. Otherwise, the dead man's relatives will
> kill him." So now YAHWEH said to Joshua, "Tell
> the people of Israel to choose these cities of asy-
> lum as I instructed you through Moses." (vv. 1–3)

At this point in Israel's early stages of their nationhood, God had not given the people any type of law enforcement agency. There was no marshal, sheriff, or state trooper. There was simply the law of Moses that governed the people, and the elders of the people were the ones who made sure that the people kept that law. In this case, Joshua set aside six cities of asylum into which a guilty man or woman, someone who had unintentionally killed another person, could run and find safety.

He placed three of these cities on one side of the Jordan and three on the other side of the Jordan and declared them as places of safety from the "avenger of blood" (Joshua 20:5 NIV). This "avenger of blood" is another way of saying "the law" because, in those days, it was the family of the slain person who avenged the blood. If somebody was killed, the family of the murdered person would avenge the blood guilt. In this case, the Lord gave the guilty a place in which they could take refuge. Symbolically and prophetically, all the six cities of asylum point us to Christ.

JESUS IS OUR CITY OF ASYLUM

Both the justice and mercy of God kiss in the person of Jesus Christ of Nazareth. The unique concept of the city of asylum is a wondrous representation of the Lord and his heart of love to restore the guilty back to his embrace. I want to give you a few key aspects of these six cities.

1. *They point us to Christ.* They simply and powerfully reveal to us who Jesus Christ is. Six is the number of man and is a picture of the guilt, the flesh, and the wickedness of man. And yet, in Christ, we have freedom, and we have safety. So, the cities of asylum

reveal Christ. They speak of the Lord Jesus as the answer to the problem of the sin nature.

2. *They give us, who are guilty, a free pass.* They not only point to Christ, but the cities of asylum save the guilty. They provide a hiding place, a refuge, for those who are undeserving, unprotected, and unwanted. Sound like Jesus to you?

3. *The cities of asylum were also priestly cities.* Interestingly, they were also designated as home to the Levites. Wherever there are priests (Levites), that is a place of safety. Realize this: in the New Testament, every one of us in Christ's body is a priest. We all have priestly functions, priestly duties, and priestly responsibilities. We are priests in the house of God. Since the Levites were the priestly tribe, wherever they lived, that city then would become a refuge for the guilty. What a picture! Wherever God has a priestly company interceding, praying, and blessing the city, there's a refuge there.

God wants you and me to be intercessory priests. He wants us to cover our cities. Whatever city you live in, you need to bless that city. You need to pray for that city—pray for your mayor, your city government, the business community, the police department, fire department, schools, and so on. Pray for safety, blessing, and protection. Pray against murders, crime, and filth. Take your priestly position, standing in God's house, and release your prayer covering over the city. Your city will become a city of asylum as God's people speak blessing and hope, not judgment.

4. *The cities were strategically located* (three on one side of the Jordan and three on the other). These six cities scattered around the nation became *very accessible* refuges for the people. No matter where you might have found yourself in Israel, you would never be very far from a refuge. How many of you know Jesus is accessible? We don't ever really get that far away from him, do we? He's available to us. He's near. He's a very present help to us, our close-at-hand city of asylum.

> God, you're such a safe and powerful place to
> find refuge!
> You're a proven help in time of trouble—
> more than enough and always available whenever
> I need you. (Psalm 46:1)

Isaiah said it this way: "The city is a stronghold for us" (26:1). That is so true! Jesus Christ is our strong city of asylum. God wants it to be easy for the sinners to find safety. I think it's wrong for the church of Jesus Christ to make the gospel complicated or complex. Too often, we add all of our church stuff, all of our religious stuff, all of our weird stuff, and our spiritual "hoops" that people have to jump through.

The Gospel is really just gut-level simple: come to Jesus, and do it quickly because life's going to be over before you know it. You may have a religion good enough to die by, but do you have a religion good enough to live by? Does it work for your everyday life? Jesus Christ not only gives us fire insurance, but he also gives us the sweet assurance that he's real and that he hears our prayers. He wants us to live like he's near and available. He's not a distant, angry God, but he is a soothing, comforting friend who is as near to us as any human being could ever be, even more so. Jesus *is* our refuge, and he wants us to know him that way.

THE CITIES OF ASYLUM, A WORD STUDY

Let's take a look at the six names of these cities because the meaning of each name speaks of different aspects of the Lord Jesus Christ. I'm going to take them in the order the Bible lists them in Joshua 20:7–8. Here are the six cities of asylum, their names, what they mean, and how they point us to Christ.

1. KADESH

Kadesh is the Hebrew word for "holiness" or "righteousness." Jesus is our Kadesh, our holy refuge. When we come to the Lord Jesus Christ, he clothes us in his holiness and his righteousness. Suddenly, our filthy garments, stained by sin and shame, are taken off us, and we are given the clean, fresh garments of righteousness that Jesus Christ provides. He is our holiness! Christians who try to live godly lives but do not connect to the life of Christ are living a religious myth and are in legalistic bondage. There is only one life that pleases God. It is the life of his Son. As we live that *borrowed* life of Christ, he becomes our holiness. He becomes our righteousness. In the hiding place of our Savior, we get righteousness as a precious gift. Have you come for refuge in Jesus Christ? Do you know him as Lord and Savior? Are you ready to stand before a holy God? You won't be able to do so in your own righteousness, which the Bible likens to filthy rags.

> We have all become contaminated with sin,
>   and you see our self-righteousness as nothing
>   better than a menstrual rag.
> We are all like fallen leaves,

and our sins sweep us away like the wind.
(Isaiah 64:6)

Christ alone is our hiding place and covering. In him, we don't have to be perfect because we are perfectly loved and perfectly covered.

2. SHECHEM

The next city of asylum was a city called Shechem. Now, *Shechem* is the Hebrew word for "strength" or "shoulder." This refuge was a city called "strength," a city named after a man's shoulder, the place of strength, where we place our heavy burdens. Christ Jesus is the Worthy One, the Strong One, the Capable One, the Wise One, the only One able to carry governmental authority on his shoulder (see Isaiah 9:6). So, coming to Christ is coming into a *strong refuge*. Oh friend, do you feel weak today, like you can't go on or like you just can't seem to "get it all together"? Let me tell you, Christ is a strong refuge. He's a place of hiding. He'll surround you with strength. To know him is to touch the omnipotence of God. Oh, the might and strength! We can be strong in the strength and power of his might (see Ephesians 6:10). So, the strength of God is ours as we run into this city of asylum called Shechem, our Lord Jesus.

3. HEBRON

Another city of asylum is a city called Hebron. The word *Hebron* is literally "fellowship." It's where two become one. It's where union, unity, and communion take place *in* Jesus Christ, and we enter into the realm of fellowship with God through Christ. In the book of 1 John, the apostle John writes to the church and says that if we walk in the light as God is in the light, we have fellowship with one another: "If we keep living in the pure light that surrounds him, we share unbroken fellowship with one another, and the blood of Jesus, his Son, continually cleanses us from all sin" (1 John 1:7).

We (God and the believer) have fellowship with one another. You see, fellowship is walking with God, in the light, in our city of asylum, Jesus Christ, our Hebron. He's our holy Hebron. He is the realm of fellowship. We enter into God through Christ. How would you like to see and feel and experience God from the inside instead of from far away, on the outside looking in? In Christ, we are brought into fellowship. We're brought into union with God. We become one with God in spirit: "The one who joins himself to the Lord is mingled into one spirit with him" (1 Corinthians 6:17).

He who is joined to the Lord is one spirit with him! I can be in the jungle. I can be driving my car. I can be asleep on my bed with my head upon my fluffy pillow, and I can have intimate fellowship with the living God. That's so glorious. People can't take that away from you. The devil can't take that away, and, friend, bad circumstances can't take it away either. There is fellowship with God available for us no matter where we are or what we are going through. If you're sick in your body, let me tell you, Jesus Christ wants to bring you into divine union and into his divine strength. He'll carry you on his shoulder and bring you into a realm of sweet fellowship.

4. Bezer

The next city of asylum is a place called Bezer. *Bezer* is the Hebrew word for "fortress." Jesus is our strong fortress. If we are in Christ, we are in the stronghold of his presence. I think the church makes too much of the strongholds of demonic power and not enough of the stronghold of God's love and grace. Let's focus on that stronghold! To know Jesus Christ is to come inside a fortress, a place of strength, a place of courage. Let's enter into "Bezer," where our weak soul can be made strong and the seemingly insurmountable issues of life can be rendered impotent.

5. RAMOTH

The fifth city of asylum was named Ramoth. It's the Hebrew word for "heights" or "heavenly places" or "the high place." It is a place of exaltation, a place where we are lifted up. Would you like to be lifted up above your mess? Whatever (or whoever) our problem or difficulty may be, God wants to lift us *up* and *over* it. He wants to get us out of any pit. It is the lie from the devil himself that you cannot live above depression, discouragement, despair, or suicidal thoughts. Nothing is higher than Jesus! His name is above every other name, and at his name, everything must bow (see Philippians 2:9–11). Whatever issue we face, Jesus Christ is our high refuge. He can take us up and over what we're going through this very day. Come to "Ramoth" and hide in the high place.

> He raised us up with Christ the exalted One, and
> we ascended with him into the glorious perfection
> and authority of the heavenly realm, for we are
> now co-seated as one with Christ! (Ephesians 2:6)

There is a shelter in the Most High God, lifting high the soul of man, bringing us far above the dismal clouds, far above the stars and the universe as we know it, where God dwells in "the high place," exalted with seraphim and cherubim and the four living creatures. To that realm, God wants to take you, and rest assured, sin won't catch you there. Temptation won't tackle you there. The issues that you're facing now will become so small. In that high and lofty place, God will impart his grace. God will impart the kisses of heaven, and you will face earthly battles from a heavenly perspective of victory, not defeat. What a wonderful high refuge we have in Jesus!

6. GOLAN

The last city of asylum is a place called Golan. By the act of God, Joshua designated Golan to be a city where a fugitive could go and be protected from blood guilt. Let me tell you, we all need a Golan, a hiding place. Some people hide in drugs. Some people hide in immoral relationships. Some people hide their issues and stuff them down as deep as they can, but, friend, there is only one hiding place that will satisfy your soul. It's the Lord Jesus Christ, our place of perfection.

The meaning of the word *Golan* is debated by Hebrew scholars, but most believe that it means "circle, to be hedged or walled in completely, a complete circle." Golan was a place to be totally encased in God. In this same way, Jesus Christ perfectly encircles us in his love, and all evil is kept outside. There's a Scripture verse in the prophets that says God has placed a wall of fire around you: "'I myself will be a wall of fire around it,' declares the LORD, 'and I will be its glory within'" (Zechariah 2:5 NIV).

If the enemy is going to come in, he's going to have to go through that fire and get burned up! You are protected and safe, and you don't have to fear evil tidings or bad news in Golan. You don't have to fear for your own life. You don't have to carry anxieties about your job, your relationships, or your future because in Christ Jesus, our strong refuge, we are kept safe, surrounded by his perfection. We're walled in. We're hedged all around with grace and mercy. Hallelujah!

THE BIG PICTURE

I believe the six names of these cities, when taken collectively, also paint a picture for us. When we link each one together like a strand of pearls, this is what we come up with:

- Kadesh—holiness, righteousness
- Shechem—strength
- Hebron—fellowship
- Bezer—exalted, lifted up
- Ramoth—fortress
- Golan—encircled

He gives us his *righteousness*, then he imparts his *strength* and brings us into *fellowship.* He makes us secure by *lifting* us up on high in the *fortress* of his presence, where he finally *encircles* us in his perfect love and grace, forever.

You see, Jesus Christ is leading us into the beautiful refuge of his presence. Where are we going to run when we are guilty, alone, uncovered, and in need? We run heedlessly into the strong arms of a Savior, our city of asylum, the Lord Jesus Christ. The Bible concludes in the book of Revelation with a sad picture of the ungodly inhabitants of the earth, even the kings and princes running in fear saying, "Fall on us at once! Hide us quickly from the glorious face of the one seated on the throne and from the wrath of the Lamb" (Revelation 6:16). Everybody is going to look for a hiding place in those last days, but it won't be found anywhere but in Christ. No earthly solace can offer true strength, joy, peace, fellowship, or exaltation. Only Jesus gives us the spiritual buoyancy that lifts us and carries us through all of life's ups and downs. We can run to him and there find all we ever needed or wanted, and so much more.

Jesus truly is a stronghold for the helpless. He exalts the humble, gives us power when we're tempted, and carries us on his shoulder when we're weary. He is the true place of fellowship for every lonely person, every widow, and every orphan. He provides safety for us, not just one day or one week or one month or one year, but all the time, for all of our lives, for all eternity. Jesus Christ is our city of asylum forever and ever.

Enter into Jesus, Your Safe Refuge

I want to ask you, dear reader, if there anything you need to make right with God. Is there any issue you need to settle between yourself and Jesus? Do you know him as your King? Do you know him as your hiding place, your personal city of asylum? The healthy don't need a physician, and the innocent don't need a savior, but how about you? Are you guilty? If you feel the shame of sin in your life and the weight of issues you can't overcome, I say to you, *Jesus Christ is help for the guilty.* He is hope for the despairing. He is love for the broken and shattered. He is peace for the troubled and those burdened with anxious care. Don't let another moment go by without running into his arms. Let him wash your guilt away today and give you his glory.

LET'S PRAY

Lord, there is no other name under heaven, given among men, whereby we must be saved but only the name of Jesus Christ. You are my city of asylum. You are the One I run into when I am in pain, under pressure, feeling tempted, or weighed down with weariness. It's you, Lord Jesus, who gives me peace. It's you who satisfies my soul. It's you, Lord, who lifts me up on high and kisses me in fellowship for eternity. It's you, Lord, who gives me strength in my weakness. When I am grieving, when I am in pain in my body or in my soul, it's you who gives me comfort, peace, and joy. I call you my refuge. You are the place where I hide. I want to run into your arms, into your presence, into the joy of your resurrection, Lord. In this moment, I come. I let go of all other safety nets and backup plans. I surrender all other things I have run into for help and comfort, and I come to you, Lord Jesus, in full surrender and assurance. Thank you for your love. Amen.

ENDNOTES

1   Joshua 1:9. God gave Joshua seven promises: (1) He would possess a vast territory (see vv. 3–4). (2) No one would be able to defeat him (see v. 5). (3) God would be with him as he was with Moses (see v. 5). (4) God would never fail him (see v. 5). (5) God would never abandon him (see v. 5). (6) He would enjoy prosperity and success (see v. 8). (7) God would be with him wherever he went (see v. 6). Remember, what God promised Joshua, he also promises you.

2   We all have a purpose and a destiny upon our lives whether we know it or not. Truly our purpose is to fulfill the will of God for our lives, but in order to do that, we have to know what the will of God is and then begin to walk in it. We enter into God's will for our life when we receive Jesus Christ, God's Son, as our Savior. He then leads and guides us into the perfect will of God (see Romans 12:1–2).

3   Joshua 1:8. Or "meditate," "ponder," "imagine," "mutter," or "talk to oneself." See Psalm 1:2; Proverbs 3:1–2.

4   Flax is the source of linen cloth. The priest of the Bible and

Jesus himself wore a linen cloth. In fact, Jesus was wrapped in linen cloths as a baby and in a linen burial robe at his death. In a sense, the spies hidden under flax is a hint of our lives being hidden in the righteousness of Christ.

5   The tributaries of the Jordan, swollen with the spring snowmelt from Mount Hermon, flooded the river valley. The width of the flooding river could have been up to a mile at the time of the miracle-crossing. (See 1 Chronicles 12:15.) By comparing Joshua 3:14–15; 4:19 with Exodus 9:31, we learn that Israel's miracle-crossing took place in the spring when both barley and flax were harvested, four days before Passover.

6   Joshua 3:3. The ark is the center of this story. It is mentioned or alluded to twenty-one (or 3×7) times in Joshua 3 and 4. Twenty-one, in the language of biblical numbers, signifies a complete manifestation of God. The ark is a wonderful picture of our Lord Jesus Christ. The power of Christ within us enables us to pass over into our full inheritance. Jesus, our forerunner, leads us in. The ark was a constant reminder that God is powerful, holy, and to be obeyed. The ark also symbolizes God's mercy, for it had a mercy seat as a lid, or cover. Jesus is our Mercy Seat, or atoning sacrifice (see 1 John 2:2). Notice that it wasn't only the ark (Jesus) that went into the dry riverbed but also all of Israel. In the same manner, every believer today is co-crucified

with Christ (see Galatians 2:20), and our "Adam-nature" was dismantled by the work of the cross (see Romans 6:6).

7 Joshua 3:4. The Hebrew word *derek* can mean "way" or "manner." They were to march in a new manner—with their eyes on the ark (see Colossians 1:10). A new order for a new day. Before they crossed the Jordan, the ark had always been covered. Beginning when they crossed the Jordan and entered the promised land, the ark was in plain sight. In the Old Testament, Jesus was concealed; in the New Testament, Jesus is revealed. Without all the covering, the weight on the priests' shoulders would have been less. See Matthew 11:28–30.

8 Joshua 3:5. Some scholars are puzzled over the use of the plural word for miracles when it was only one miracle (parting the river). The plural implied the beginning of a new season of miracles and wonders as they crossed over.

9 Joshua 3:17. The miracle-crossing of the Jordan bore many similarities to the parting of the Red Sea. (1) Both involved water. (2) Both were witnessed by the entire nation of Israel. (3) Both involved an act of a servant of God— Moses stretched out his rod over the water, and Joshua commanded the priests and the people. (4) Both removed a barrier to the forward advance of God's people. (5) Both

miracles vindicated God's leader (see Exodus 14:31; Joshua 4:14). (6) Both required the obedience of God's people (see Exodus 14:15; Joshua 3:3). (7) Both miracles enabled Israel to cross over on dry ground (see Exodus 14:22). (8) Both miracles were performed while God's people stood still (see Exodus 14:14; footnote on Joshua 3:8). (9) Both the waters of the Red Sea and of the Jordan were restored to their places. (10) Both miracles became a hinge of history, marking a new beginning. (11) Both miracles revealed God's tremendous power to defeat his enemies. (12) Both miracles resulted in songs of praise (see Exodus 15; Psalm 114; Habakkuk 3).

10   Joshua 5:2. Circumcision, the cutting off of the foreskin from the penis, was the sign of the covenant that God made with Abraham (see Genesis 17:9–14). The reason for doing this is given in Joshua 5:4–7. The male children born while Israel was wandering in the wilderness for forty years had not been circumcised. This would leave Israel vulnerable for a number of days as the men healed.

11   Joshua 5:2. Or "the second time." All male Israelites had been circumcised before their exodus from Egypt (see Exodus 12:44–51), so this would be the nation's second time.

12 Joshua 5:3. Or "Gibeath Haaraloth." *Gibeath Haaraloth* means "Hill of Foreskins." There could have been more than a half million men who were circumcised at that time. The Hebrew word for "circumcision" is *muwl*, which means "to cut short," "to blunt," "to destroy," or "to cut in pieces." The principle of circumcision is that the flesh (human nature apart from divine influence) must be cut off and removed if God's people are to enter into the fullness of their spiritual inheritance (see Colossians 2:10–11; 3:9). Circumcision was performed on the eighth day after birth (see Luke 2:21). Eight is the number of a new beginning. The circumcision of the heart (see Deuteronomy 10:16; 30:6; Jeremiah 4:4; Romans 2:29) frees us to hear from God, to live in the Spirit of God (see Philippians 3:3), and to enter into the fullness of God (see Romans 6:1–14).

13 Howard Taylor and Mrs. Howard Taylor, *Hudson Taylor and the China Inland Mission: The Growth of a Work of God* (London: Morgan and Scott, 1919), 355.

14 E. A. Hoffman, "I Must Tell Jesus," written 1894, Hymnary. org, accessed April 1, 2022, https://hymnary.org/text/i_must_tell_jesus_all_of_my_trials.

15 Joshua 10:3. *Hoham* means "driven [forced]" or "he

crushed." He ruled as king of Hebron, twenty miles south of Jerusalem. *Hebron* means "alliance."

16 Joshua 10:3. *Piram* means "wild donkey" or "fierce." Piram ruled as king of Jarmuth (modern Khirbet el-Yarmuk), which is eighteen miles southwest of Jerusalem. *Jarmuth* means "high place." These high places could also include "every arrogant attitude that is raised up in defiance of the true knowledge of God" (2 Corinthians 10:5).

17 Joshua 10:3. *Japhia* means "one who enlightens" or "elevated." Japhia ruled as king of Lachish, fifteen miles west of Hebron. *Lachish* means "invincible." Archeologists believe that Tell el-Hesy is ancient Lachish.

18 Joshua 10:3. *Debir* means "speaker" or "oracle." Debir was the king of Eglon, ten miles west of Hebron. *Eglon* means "young bull."

19 Joshua 10:6. The five kings occupied the high ground, standing above everyone else. Their elevated position is a picture of pride in a perceived higher status. Many believers today look down on others who are not like themselves. See Isaiah 40:4; Philippians 2:5–10; 3 John 9–10.

20 Joshua 10:12. *Aijalon* means "field of deer" or "a strong

place." The fiery passion of the Lord (see Isaiah 9:7; 37:32) consumed Joshua as he spoke to the sun and moon so he could finish the fight. What faith we see in his decree! Imagine if that zeal came upon you.

21   Joshua 10:13. Or "Jashar." See 2 Samuel 1:18. Jashar is from the Hebrew word *yashar*, which means "upright," "correct," or "pleasing." The scroll's name can also be translated "the Song of Heroes" or "the True Record." The *Scroll of the Upright One* was a book likely containing war songs, prayers, and exploits of Israel. The Jewish sage Rashi believed "Jashar" was a symbolic name for the Torah. Others believe it is the same as the book of the wars of the Lord (see Numbers 21:14). There has been no manuscript found containing the *Scroll of the Upright One*. There are other books by that name, but they are not the same as the one mentioned here.

22   See Appendix 1 for a list of the thirty-one kings in Joshua 12 that Joshua conquered.

23   The name of God, El (Mighty God), according to its gematria (the numerical value in Jewish culture), equals thirty-one. Only the Mighty God can conquer these warring kings who fight with us within our hearts.

ABOUT THE AUTHORS

BRIAN & CANDICE SIMMONS have been described as true pioneers in ministry. Their teaching and spiritual gifts have opened doors into several nations to bring the message of authentic awakening and revival to many. For many years, they have labored together to present Christ in his fullness wherever God sends them.

After a dramatic conversion to Christ in 1971, Brian and Candice answered the call of God to leave everything behind and become missionaries to unreached peoples. Taking their three children to the jungle tropical rain forest of Central America, they planted churches for many years with the Paya-Kuna people group.

After their ministry overseas, Brian and Candice returned to North America, where they planted numerous ministries, including a dynamic church in New England (US). They also established Passion & Fire Ministries, under which they travel full-time as Bible teachers in service of local churches throughout the world.

Brian and Candice are co-authors of numerous books, Bible studies, and devotionals that help readers encounter God's heart and experience a deeper revelation of God as our Bridegroom-King, including The Blessing, The Image Maker, The Sacred Journey, The Wilderness, and Throne Room Prayer.

Brian is also the lead translator of The Passion Translation®. The Passion Translation (TPT) is a heart-level translation that uses Hebrew, Greek, and Aramaic manuscripts to express God's fiery heart of love to this generation, merging the emotion and life-changing truth of God's Word.

Brian and Candice have been married since 1971 and have three children as well as precious grandchildren and great-grand-children. Their passion is to live as loving examples of a spiritual father and mother to this generation.